THE NEWSROUND BOOK OF
SPACE

NICK HEATHCOTE
MARSHALL CORWIN
SUSIE STAPLES

BBC BOOKS

THE AUTHORS

This book has been written by three members of the production team on BBC TV's popular *Newsround*. Nick Heathcote, the programme editor, is also a co-author of the best-selling *Blue Peter Green Book* (BBC Books 1990). Marshall Corwin, a co-author of the *Factfinder Book of Pets* (BBC Books 1989), and Susie Staples are both producers on *Newsround*.

Published by BBC Books,
a division of BBC Enterprises Limited,
Woodlands, 80 Wood Lane, London W12 0TT
This paperback edition first published 1993

© Nick Heathcote, Marshall Corwin, Susie Staples 1992

ISBN 0 563 40309 8

Designer: Phil Kay
Picture researcher: Sally Williams
Set in Plantin by Ace Filmsetting Ltd, Frome, Somerset
Cover photographs courtesy of Nasa; back cover illustration, top right,
David A. Hardy.

Printed and bound in Belgium by Proost NV
Colour separation by Dot Gradations, Chelmsford
Cover printed by Proost NV, Belgium

CB233398
£9.99
GASTONS
SMC

About this book

PEOPLE have dreamt about space travel for centuries, but it is only recently that we have developed the technology that allows us to leave our planet and explore worlds other than our own.

On 12 April 1961, the Soviet cosmonaut Yuri Gagarin became the first man in history to escape Earth's gravity, and manned space flight finally became a reality. Eight years later, in 1969, Neil Armstrong and Buzz Aldrin landed on the moon. Less than 12 years after that, in 1981, re-usable shuttles began flying astronauts (the American equivalent of cosmonauts) to space and back on a regular basis. Just before Christmas 1988, two cosmonauts, Vladimir Titov and Musa Manarov, returned to Earth after spending a whole year of their lives in space. These are just a few of the many from around the world who have earned a place in space's Hall of Fame.

The Newsround Book of Space looks back at the amazing achievements of recent years, and highlights some of the events that led up to them. It describes in detail what is happening in the world of space today: how an astronaut is trained; what it is like to live aboard a space station; how rockets and space probes work.

It also takes you on a fantastic voyage into the future of space travel – a voyage that will take human beings back to the moon, to Mars . . . and beyond.

Contents

In this book...

The Newsround Book of Space, packed with colour pictures and detailed illustrations, contains all you've ever wanted to know about the past, present and future of space travel.

SPACE SHUTTLES

The invention of the re-usable shuttle marked a new era in the history of space, promising cheap and reliable travel. But has it been as successful as was first hoped? (See pages 20–25.)

ROCKETS

The conquest of space has been made possible by powerful rockets, capable of blasting into orbit at speeds of around 30,000 km (20,000 miles) per hour. (See pages 10–13.)

ASTRONAUTS

Many apply but few are chosen. What is it really like to be an astronaut in space? What sort of training does he or she go through in preparation for a mission? (See pages 26–35.)

UNMANNED CRAFT

Many craft sent into space are remote controlled, beaming vital information back to Earth. Space probes have visited almost every planet in our solar system. (See pages 42–51.)

SPACE STATIONS

Highly equipped science laboratories are in orbit around the Earth. Find out what kinds of experiments are carried out in them, and why the space scientists' work is so important. (See pages 36–41.)

THE FUTURE

The future looks even more exciting than the past. A permanent space station has been given the go-ahead and there are plans for bases on the moon and Mars. One day people might live in giant space cities! (See pages 66–73.)

ALIENS

Books, comics and films about space contain extraordinary visions of life beyond our planet. What are the chances that creatures like E.T. really exist? (See pages 74–81.)

SPACE ON EARTH

You can experience space on Earth in the world's top space museums. Or learn what it's like to be an astronaut in specially built space camps. (See pages 82–87.)

LANDMARKS

Space travel has been packed full of stunning, earth-shattering moments. (See pages 90–95 for a space log charting these historic events.)

Our solar system

L ESS than 400 years ago, most people still believed the Earth was the centre of the universe. The turning-point came when an Italian scientist, Galileo Galilei, constructed the first astronomical telescope in 1609. For the first time it was possible to see what the moon really looked like close up. Galileo's studies of the night sky proved that the Earth, along with the other planets in our solar system, rotates round the sun.

We know now that our sun is just one of millions of stars in the galaxy called the Milky Way. And that the Milky Way is one of countless galaxies in the universe.

Galileo Galilei, who made the first astronomical telescope. Today, many instruments help us to learn about the universe and our solar system.

PERSPECTIVE ON THE PLANETS

	DIAMETER	APPROX. DISTANCE FROM SUN
Mercury	4880 km (3030 miles)	58m km (36m miles)
Venus	12,100 km (7516 miles)	108m km (67m miles)
Earth	12,756 km (7921 miles)	150m km (93m miles)
Mars	6790 km (4220 miles)	228m km (141m miles)
Jupiter	142,800 km (88,700 miles)	778m km (483m miles)
Saturn	120,000 km (74,000 miles)	1427m km (886m miles)
Uranus	52,000 km (32,500 miles)	2870m km (1780m miles)
Neptune	49,000 km (30,700 miles)	4497m km (2790m miles)
Pluto	2300 km (1400 miles)	5900m km (3700m miles) (average)

SUN The biggest and brightest star in our sky; our main energy source

MERCURY Scorching hot, rocky and covered in craters; no air or water

VENUS The easiest planet to spot because it is so bright; extremely hot

EARTH Two-thirds covered by water – the key to life; one moon

MARS The 'red planet'; more like Earth than any other planet; two moons

JUPITER Giant ball of gas; 16 moons; our solar system's biggest planet

SATURN 10 known moons; three rings made from millions of lumps of rock and ice

URANUS Green and plain; rings; 15 moons; only visible through a telescope

NEPTUNE Bluish globe of gas; two rings; eight moons

PLUTO Our smallest planet; sometimes closer than Neptune to the sun; one moon

SUN

MERCURY

VENUS

EARTH

MARS

JUPITER

Space rocks

There's more to our solar system than the nine known planets. Thousands of lumps of rock, known as asteroids, orbit the sun between Jupiter and Mars. When a fragment of space rock burns up as it enters our atmosphere it is known as a meteor or, sometimes, a shooting star. If it crashes through Earth's atmosphere and makes a hole in the ground it is called a meteorite. We can see the glow of comets when these frozen lumps of rock and gas get too close to the sun.

Space telescopes and probes and radio telescopes provide information about the universe. This is an artist's impression of the radio telescope at Jodrell Bank, Cheshire.

Getting off the ground

THE Chinese invented the explosive mixture that fired the first rockets more than 1000 years ago. They concocted a 'black powder' which exploded when lit, and created bright sparks and a loud bang. These were the world's first fireworks.

Later, the Chinese used their secret recipe to fire arrows at their enemies. But it took hundreds of years before their important invention travelled west to Europe, where the once-guarded formula was copied to make gunpowder for weapons of war. It was the end of the nineteenth century before scientists realised for sure that rocket technology could be used to go to space.

German breakthrough The rocket glider was flown in Germany before the end of the 1920s. Gliders had been flown since the beginning of the twentieth century, and a rocket was used to give this version a powerful boost. It used solid fuel and flew for about 1½ km (1 mile) in just over a minute.

Rocket mania People in the West were mad about rockets during the 1920s and there were some harebrained experiments. Some of the more crazy inventions ended in disaster. But it was all in the quest for knowledge and to achieve the ultimate goal of getting into space.

Russian pioneer Many people believe Konstantin Tsiolkovsky (above) was the father of space travel. At the beginning of this century, he designed rockets and spaceships and worked out how to get them into space.

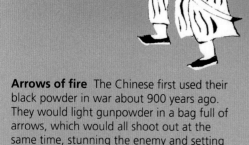

Arrows of fire The Chinese first used their black powder in war about 900 years ago. They would light gunpowder in a bag full of arrows, which would all shoot out at the same time, stunning the enemy and setting the ground alight wherever they landed.

Sir Isaac and the apple In 1665, the British scientist Sir Isaac Newton (above) was the first person to understand gravity. By watching an apple fall from a tree, he realised there was a strong force that pulled everyone and everything on Earth towards the ground.

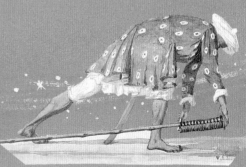

Weapons of war By the late eighteenth century, rocket-fired weapons were being used in India. Gunpowder was cased in iron and attached to a rod of bamboo. It was lit and thrown by hand. Soldiers from Britain were attacked by these weapons – and took them home to copy!

American pioneer In the United States, Robert Goddard was the great pioneer of rockets. He is pictured here with the world's first liquid-fuelled rocket which he launched successfully in 1926. Although it only flew for a few seconds, it marked an important stage in the history of space flight.

Mass production Sir William Congreve (above) was a British soldier who improved on the Indian rockets in the early nineteenth century. Congreve rockets were produced in huge numbers and used successfully in many battles.

From war to peace The V2 was a deadly rocket used by the Germans in the Second World War to attack London. After the war some of its German designers settled in the United States. Here they are in 1950 launching a V2 at Cape Canaveral, Florida, now one of the world's most important launching sites for space travel.

Blast-off!

TO stay in orbit spacecraft and satellites must reach the phenomenal speed of 28,000 km (17,500 miles) per hour. So the rockets that launch them need to be extremely powerful. Rockets don't fly like aeroplanes, which rely on air rushing past their wings to lift them off the ground. Instead, they roar straight upwards by pushing out vast amounts of hot gas with great force. This means they can also operate in the vacuum of space.

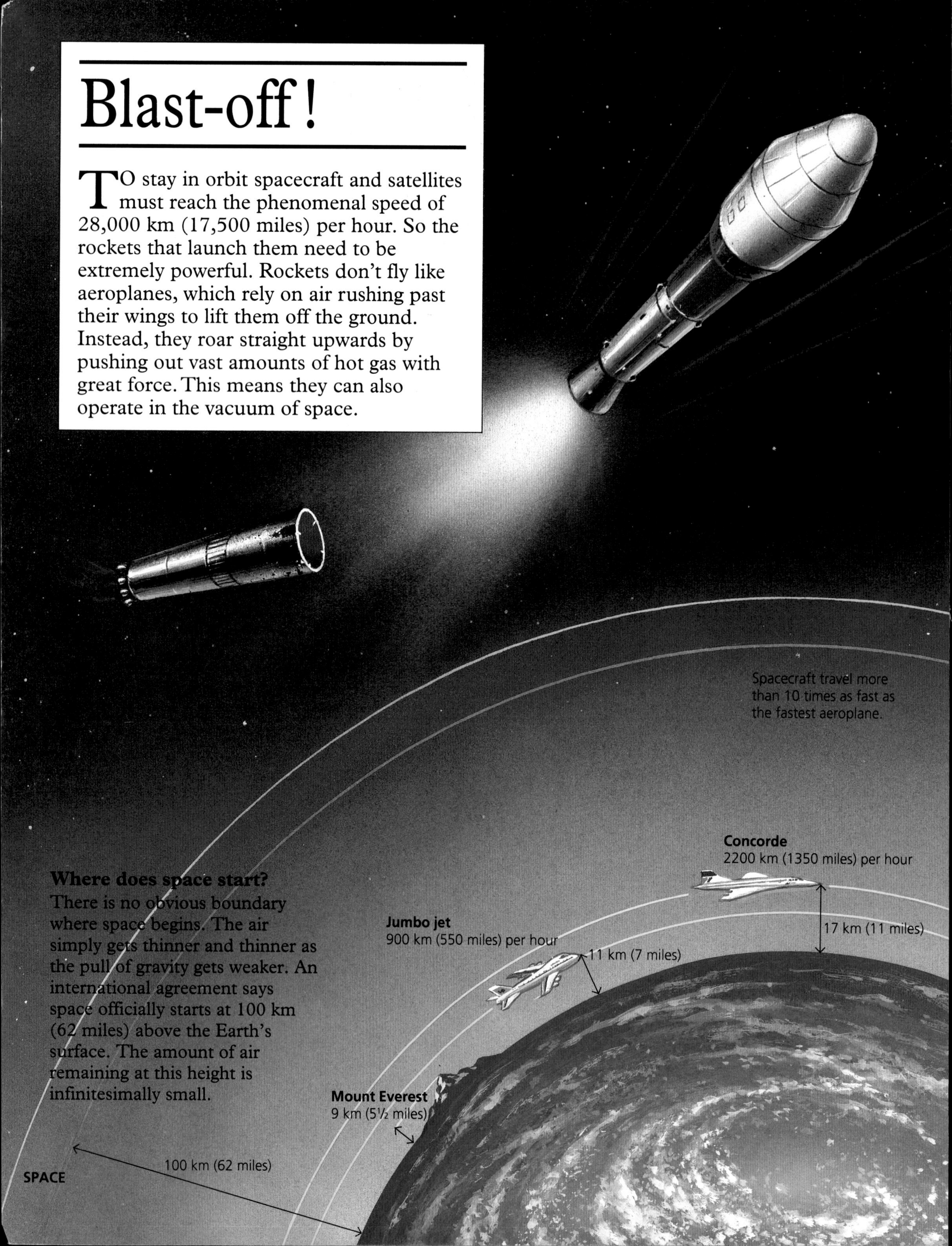

Spacecraft travel more than 10 times as fast as the fastest aeroplane.

Concorde
2200 km (1350 miles) per hour

17 km (11 miles)

Jumbo jet
900 km (550 miles) per hour

11 km (7 miles)

Where does space start?
There is no obvious boundary where space begins. The air simply gets thinner and thinner as the pull of gravity gets weaker. An international agreement says space officially starts at 100 km (62 miles) above the Earth's surface. The amount of air remaining at this height is infinitesimally small.

Mount Everest
9 km (5½ miles)

100 km (62 miles)

SPACE

Rocket stages

Rockets used for space launches are usually made up of two or three separate sections, known as stages (see p. 14), to help provide enough power to reach orbit. Each stage fires in turn and then falls away after a few minutes when it runs out of fuel. In this way the rocket gets lighter and lighter allowing it to reach great speed as it approaches the borders of space. Some launchers, like the space shuttle and the Soviet Soyuz rocket (right), have extra 'strap-on' rocket boosters at their side.

Spacecraft
28,000 km (17,500 miles) per hour

ORBIT

If speed drops, spacecraft starts to fall back to Earth.

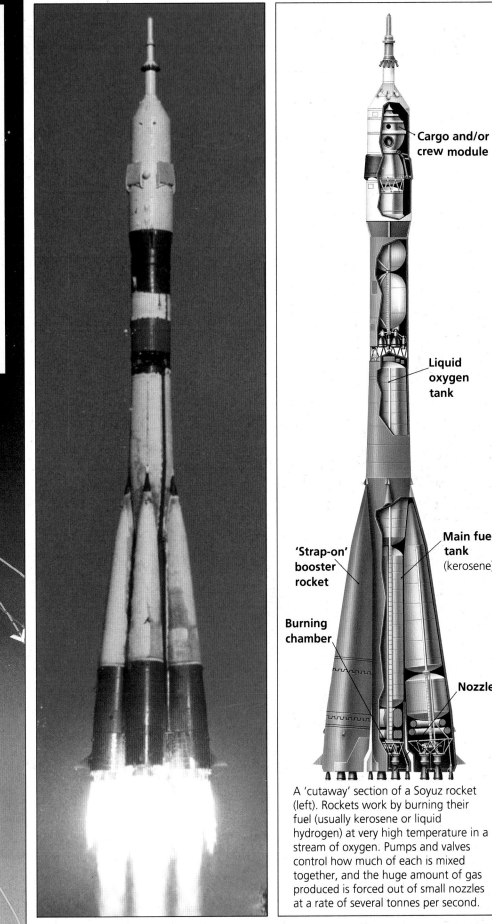

Cargo and/or crew module

Liquid oxygen tank

'Strap-on' booster rocket

Main fuel tank (kerosene)

Burning chamber

Nozzle

A 'cutaway' section of a Soyuz rocket (left). Rockets work by burning their fuel (usually kerosene or liquid hydrogen) at very high temperature in a stream of oxygen. Pumps and valves control how much of each is mixed together, and the huge amount of gas produced is forced out of small nozzles at a rate of several tonnes per second.

We've got the power!

Rockets have got bigger and more powerful during the twentieth century, and some of the most significant are shown below. Most powerful of all is the Soviet Energiya, which can lift a cargo of almost 200 tonnes into orbit. Even so, like all present-day rockets, most of its weight is made up of fuel: several thousand tonnes is carried at launch.

The next era of space travel awaits a far more efficient way of getting off the ground. This may be some kind of space plane which flies to the borders of space like an aeroplane and only then switches to rocket power to blast into orbit.

This spectacular night launch of the mighty Saturn V rocket marked the end of an era: it carried three Apollo 17 astronauts on America's last manned mission to the moon in 1972.

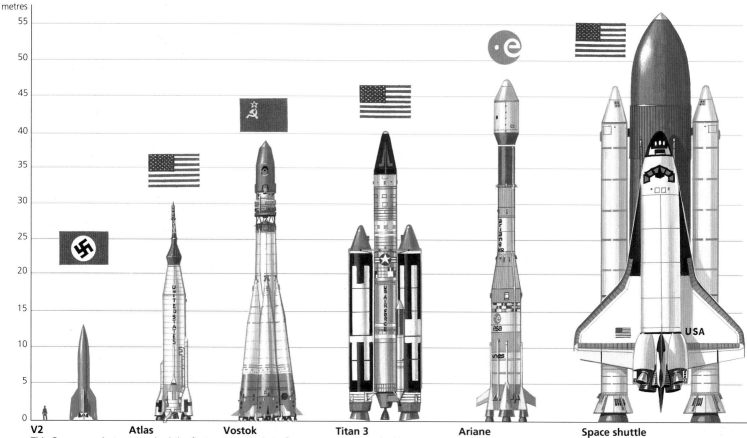

V2
This German rocket carried a bomb in its nose and was first used in attacks on London in 1944, during the Second World War, killing thousands of people.

Atlas
Launched the first American into orbit in 1962 (John Glenn). The human 'cargo' and his Mercury spacecraft weighed less than 1½ tonnes.

Vostok
Launched the first man into space in 1961 (Yuri Gagarin). It was so successful that the Soviet space programme has always used similar rockets.

Titan 3
First launched in 1964, this is America's most powerful unmanned rocket for launching satellites. Latest versions can carry a cargo of 17 tonnes.

Ariane
Europe's highly successful satellite launchers have been operating since 1979. A new version, Ariane 5, planned for 1995 will carry 15 tonnes into orbit.

Space shuttle
America's revolutionary launcher first flew in 1981. Almost everything is re-usable, but it has nevertheless failed in its aim to provide a cheaper way of launching satellites. It can deliver about 25 tonnes into orbit.

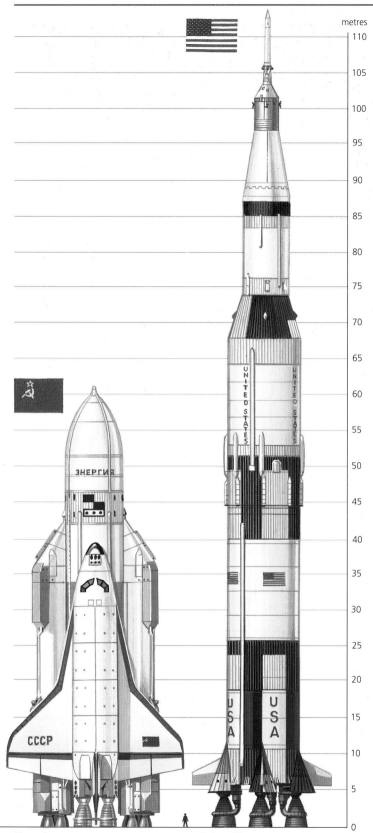

Return to Earth

Before the space shuttle was built American astronauts returned to Earth in only a tiny part of the original rocket. Soviet cosmonauts still use this system.

Re-entry Friction caused by ploughing into the Earth's atmosphere at 27,000 km (17,000 miles) per hour raises the temperature of the craft's protective heatshield to more than 1000°C (1800°F).

Splashdown Once safely back in the atmosphere, the craft's parachutes open to slow it down. American astronauts always splashed down in the sea, while Soviet craft usually come down over land firing retro-rockets just before landing to cushion the impact.

Energiya
The Soviet version of the space shuttle was first launched in 1987. Extra 'strap-on' boosters enable it to carry a cargo of almost 200 tonnes into space if the 'plane' is unhitched and left on Earth.

Saturn V
Dwarfs any other rocket ever built. Designed for America's Apollo moon missions (see p. 14). It flew from 1967 to 1973 and could carry 150 tonnes into Earth orbit.

Recovery Ground crews track the path of the spacecraft and are quickly on the scene to help the crew (who may be quite unsteady on their feet after a long period of weightlessness).

The race for the moon

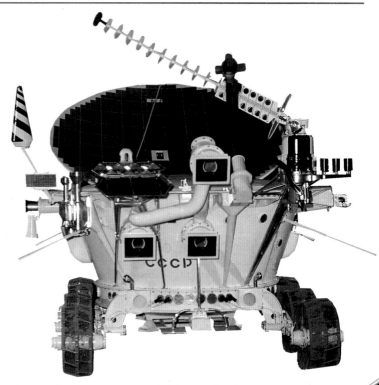

WHEN Yuri Gagarin orbited the Earth in spring 1961, the Soviet Union won a frantic race to launch the first human into space. American pride was badly dented by the news and the United States President, John F. Kennedy, responded by setting what many thought was an impossible target: 'To land a man on the moon and return him safely to Earth . . . before the decade is over!' Just eight years later, in July 1969, America's Apollo 11 moon mission triumphed – one of the greatest human achievements of all time.

Above: After America's remarkable lunar landing the Soviet Union pretended they had never wanted to send a man to the moon! A year later, in 1970, they landed this extraordinary-looking robot device on the lunar surface. Called a Lunokhod, it roved around taking pictures and carrying out experiments. Television cameras on the front allowed it to be driven by remote control from Earth.

Right: Throughout the 1960s many Soviet and American unmanned probes were sent to the moon. Some took detailed pictures like this one from lunar orbit, while others landed on the surface to check out possible landing sites for a future manned mission.

Stage 1 rocket
Fired for just 2½ minutes using 13 tonnes of fuel every second! Lifted Saturn V to a height of about 60 km (40 miles) and a speed of 9000 km (5500 miles) per hour before falling away into a remote part of the ocean.

The mighty Saturn V
It needed a giant rocket to send three astronauts plus all oxygen and supplies on their Apollo missions to the moon: each trip lasted between 8 and 12 days. When the three-stage Saturn V blasted off it weighed around 3000 tonnes, most of it made up of fuel. Only the three small craft in the nose, weighing a total of 50 tonnes, would head for the moon itself.

Lunar module
Used by two astronauts to descend the last 110 km (70 miles) from lunar orbit on to the moon. There was no need for it to be streamlined as it had no atmosphere to travel through. Ditched in space before the return journey to Earth.

Escape tower
An emergency rocket designed to pull the astronaut's command module clear if the main rocket caught fire or exploded.

Command module
The cramped 'home' of the three Apollo astronauts during their 1½ million km (1 million mile) trip. The only part of the whole spacecraft to return to Earth!

Stage 2 rocket
Fired for six minutes, taking Saturn V to 180 km (110 miles) and a speed of 25,000 km (15,500 miles) per hour before also separating and falling away.

Stage 3 rocket
Fired for two minutes to reach an orbiting speed of 28,000 km (17,500 miles) per hour at a height of 190 km (120 miles). After a few Earth orbits it fired again for five minutes to send the Apollo mission towards the moon at 40,000 km (25,000 miles) per hour. Finally ditched in space.

Service module
Supplied the astronauts with oxygen, electricity and water. Ditched in space before re-entry into the Earth's atmosphere.

A more detailed illustration of the command, service and lunar modules is on p. 56.

APOLLO 11

Humans were here! This astronaut's footprint will remain for ever in the lunar soil, as the moon has no wind or rain to disturb it. (The moon has no atmosphere – the pull of its gravity is too weak.)

'That's one small step for a man, one giant leap for mankind!' These were the famous words of Neil Armstrong on 20 July 1969, as he became the first man in history to step on to the surface of another world. (This picture is actually of Buzz Aldrin, the second man on the moon – nobody was there to take a photograph of Neil Armstrong as he stepped down!) The two astronauts planted the US flag and stayed on the moon for nearly a whole Earth day.

Man on the moon

ONLY 12 men have ever walked on the moon, all of them United States astronauts from the six Apollo missions which flew between 1969 and 1972. Each crew spent up to three days on the lunar surface, carrying out experiments and collecting samples of moon rock to bring back to Earth. It is estimated that the Apollo Project cost America a total of $25 billion!

Right: The Lunar Rover, a battery-powered buggy, was used during the last three missions to travel many kilometres from the landing site. Astronauts on foot found hopping like a kangaroo was the best way to get around (they were only one-sixth of their usual weight because of the moon's weak gravity)!

Below: The astronauts found a barren, silent world where the sky is always black and the wind never blows. The flag being saluted by the astronaut is held up with wire!

Apollo 11 astronaut Buzz Aldrin, photographed by first-man-on-the-moon Neil Armstrong (who can be seen reflected in the visor, standing next to the lunar module).

Right: Blast-off from the moon – always a tense moment as the lunar module only had one rocket engine. If it failed the crew would be left stranded.

Below: The plaque left on the moon by Apollo 17. Many other signs of human life can also be found, including the three Lunar Rovers and the wreckage of various old rockets (deliberately crashed on to the moon to stop them being a hazard in space).

HERE MAN COMPLETED HIS FIRST
EXPLORATIONS OF THE MOON
DECEMBER 1972, A.D.
MAY THE SPIRIT OF PEACE IN WHICH WE CAME
BE REFLECTED IN THE LIVES OF ALL MANKIND

EUGENE A. CERNAN
ASTRONAUT

RONALD E. EVANS
ASTRONAUT

HARRISON H. SCHMITT
ASTRONAUT

RICHARD NIXON
PRESIDENT, UNITED STATES OF AMERICA

A special tool was used to collect rock samples, as astronauts couldn't bend in their bulky spacesuits. Altogether 380 kg (840 lb) of moon rock and soil was brought to Earth to be analysed.

The loneliest man in the universe! While two men explored the moon, capturing the attention of the world, one astronaut always remained behind in lunar orbit aboard the command module.

Leaving the moon

1. The lunar module lifts off from the moon . . .

2. . . . and docks with the orbiting command module.

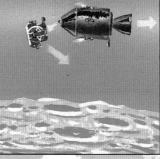

3. The lunar module is ditched and left to crash into the moon's surface . . .

4. . . . while the astronauts turn the craft round and head for home.

Our fragile Earth

THE conquest of space has meant we've been able to see our solar system in a totally new way, and have been able to capture spectacular views on film . . . not just of other planets but of Earth itself. Just the right distance from the sun for water to be liquid, two-thirds of its surface is covered by sea. No wonder astronauts call it the 'Blue Planet'.

We can marvel at its beauty. But we are now also able to study the damage people have done to our fragile planet, the home of countless living things. Hopefully, we can do something to right the wrong.

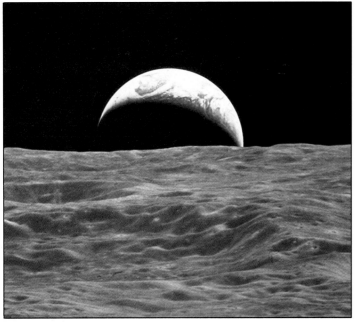

The American astronauts on Apollo 17 took this spectacular photograph of a crescent Earth rising above the lunar horizon during the final mission to the moon.

Look again! It isn't the moon rising at night. It's Earth rise! This is what the astronauts on board Apollo 16 saw as they orbited the moon. They took this snapshot of home with a hand-held camera.

As Earth rises higher on the moon's horizon, you can begin to make out the outlines of some countries. But as the Apollo 11 astronauts looked back, they could see it was a pretty cloudy day back home.

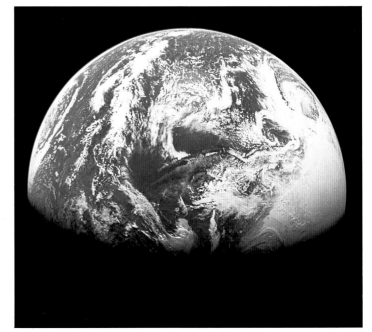

The Apollo 13 astronauts took this picture during their ill-fated moon mission in 1970 (see p. 56). It is almost a 'full Earth' now. It is cloudy, but parts of the United States are visible.

The photograph above was taken by the Apollo 17 astronauts – the last people to land on the moon – and shows a 'full Earth' seen from space. It's what visitors from another galaxy might see as they whizzed through the cosmos in their spaceship. But would it stop them in their tracks? What would they see on this colourful planet that might tempt them to drop everything and come and pay Earth a visit?

The strangers might never have seen such an interesting looking planet. Perhaps they would know that vivid blue means a big water supply, and that blobs of green suggest life exists. But what are those strange moving swirls of white? Are they friendly? The visitors might guess from the thin haze that the planet has an atmosphere – so it might be safe to land!

For the earthlings who took this picture, the image was crystal clear. That big brown lump is the continent of Africa, and there at the bottom, not to be confused with cloud, is the freezing wilderness of Antarctica.

Space taxi

IMAGINE if you had to throw away the family car at the end of every journey! It might seem crazy but, before 1981, that is exactly what happened to all spacecraft. However, at 7 a.m. on 12 April 1981 history was made . . . the American shuttle Columbia, the first re-usable space 'plane', blasted off from the Kennedy Space Centre at Cape Canaveral in Florida on Mission STS-1. The future of space travel was changed forever.

Flight commander John Young (right) and astronaut Bob Crippen flew Columbia on its first flight.

5 . . 4 . . 3 . . 2 . . 1 . . Lift - off!
Space shuttle Columbia blasts off from the Kennedy Space Centre on 12 April 1981. It was exactly 20 years to the day since Yuri Gagarin became the first man in space.

3. Shut down main engines
After eight minutes the main engines, which have used about 300,000 litres (66,000 gallons) of fuel a minute, are shut down. The huge, empty fuel tank is separated and destroyed as it falls back to Earth.

4. OMS engines . . . Fire!
Next, two small engines are fired to boost the spacecraft's speed to 28,000 km (17,500 miles) per hour and place it in space orbit 250 km (150 miles) above Earth.

2. Abandon boosters
Two minutes after launch, and 45 km (28 miles) from Earth, the two giant booster rockets are separated and parachute into the sea to be recovered and used again.

5. Time for work
The crew carry out their tasks, which can be anything from placing new satellites in orbit to rescuing or repairing old ones or carrying out experiments.

Columbia
YOUNG · CRIPPEN

1. Blast-off!
The spacecraft rides 'piggy-back' style on a massive external fuel tank. At lift-off, its main engines and two rocket boosters produce a staggering power thrust of 3,504,060 kg (7,725,000 lb) – about the same as 140 jumbo jets!

6. Back to Earth
The shuttle is turned so that its OMS engines point in the direction of travel. The engines are fired, slowing the craft until it falls to Earth. Special tiles (see p. 23) protect it from intense heat as it re-enters the atmosphere.

We have touchdown!
The shuttle Columbia glides down on to the runway at Edwards Air Force Base in California on 14 April 1981, at the end of its maiden flight of just over two days and 36 Earth orbits. Shuttles land without engine power, using wing and tail flaps for control.

The inside story

Each shuttle orbiter (the technical term for the re-usable 'plane' that returns to Earth) contains more than 220,000 individual parts so it's just as well that it is re-usable! The orbiters are built in much the same way as ordinary aeroplanes, using high-strength aluminium alloys. Just like modern aircraft, they rely heavily on computers. The shuttle orbiter has five of them, four of which work at the same time to make sure there are no errors. It is 37.2 m (122 ft) long, with a wing span of 23.8 m (78 ft) and can carry a payload of up to 25 tonnes into space. The cargo bay is big enough to hold a train carriage and the shuttle has been nicknamed the 'space truck'. There are four orbiters in the American shuttle fleet – a fifth, Challenger, tragically exploded after lift-off in January 1986 (see p. 54).

OMS engines
Alongside the main engines are two smaller ones known as orbital manoeuvring system (OMS) engines. These put the orbiter in its correct orbit around Earth.

Main engines
The orbiter has three main engines which are used in the early stages of a launch.

Shuttle launches

Columbia
Columbia clears the tower on 8 August 1989. It was the first shuttle to go into space, in April 1981 and it's still flying today.

Challenger
Challenger blasts off on a week-long mission on 29 July 1985 with Spacelab 2 on board. Six months later, disaster struck.

Discovery
Discovery's third launch on 24 January 1985. It was the first shuttle to capture two damaged satellites and return them to Earth.

Payload bay
The payload bay can carry all sorts of things into space, including Spacelab – a fully equipped laboratory built by the European Space Agency (ESA). The laboratory is pressurised so scientists can carry out experiments in it without having to wear spacesuits. The first Spacelab mission was in November 1983.

Payload and remote manipulator arm
Up to four satellites can be carried by the orbiter at any one time. They are moved and placed into orbit by the remote manipulator system (RMS) arm which is controlled from the flight deck. The arm has even been used to rescue and repair rogue satellites.

Flight deck and crew quarters
The orbiter has a crew of up to eight astronauts and for most of the time they live and work in the front of the spacecraft. The flight deck is here with crew quarters below. These are the only pressurised (but still weightless) sections of the craft and here the astronauts can move around in shirtsleeve comfort.

Thrusters
The craft has 44 mini-thrusters, which fine-tune its orbit position.

Carbon insulation

Silica tiles
20,000 heat-resistant silica tiles, made from high quality sand, protect the orbiter from extreme temperatures of up to 1260°C (2300°F) as it re-enters our atmosphere.

Atlantis
Atlantis blasts off on its maiden flight on 3 October 1985. It carried a five-man crew on a top secret military mission.

Endeavour
Endeavour, Challenger's replacement, joins the shuttle fleet on 25 April 1991. Its first flight was in May 1992.

Buran
Buran, the Soviet Union's answer to the US shuttle, prepares for its first unmanned flight in 1988. Manned flights on board Buran are planned for 1994/5.

The shuttle – its future

Although the shuttle is re-usable, it has not provided the cheap manned space travel it promised. It was a huge setback when Challenger exploded in 1986, and the shuttle programme cost more than anyone imagined. Satellites can be launched much more cheaply on traditional rockets, so the United States has decided to cut back on the number of shuttle flights. But the craft has earned its place in history and shuttles will continue to fly. Already there are plans for tomorrow's space planes.

Left: One of the shuttle's many historic moments: the SBS-3 communications satellite spins out of its protective cradle aboard Columbia on 11 November 1982. It was the first satellite launch from an orbiting spacecraft.

Above: The first-ever picture of a shuttle, Challenger, orbiting Earth. It was taken on 22 June 1983 by a camera attached to a free-floating satellite.

Below: Challenger astronaut James Van Hoften floating 'free' in front of Solar Max. On 12 April 1984, it was the first satellite to be successfully captured, repaired and redeployed (see p. 58).

The 'bird' takes flight: Discovery causes a stir as it thunders away from the launch site at Cape Canaveral on 17 June 1985.

Space invaders

THE space shuttle's flight deck has nearly 2000 different switches, dials and controls and a pilot astronaut has to go through more than eight years of training before being allowed to fly the craft. Thousands apply every year but only a handful are chosen. First, candidates learn how to fly a normal jet aircraft. Then, after several years of study, the successful ones join a pool of astronauts to be specially trained in flying spacecraft. They learn with the help of one of the world's most expensive video games: the shuttle mission simulator (SMS), which has controls and displays that are just like those of a real shuttle. Computers generate space scenes and the simulator moves up, down and around on hydraulic ramps to give the feeling of travel. Everything that happens from 30 minutes before take-off through to landing back on Earth can be re-created. Hidden loudspeakers sound the alarm when things go wrong.

A 'fish-eye' lens view of Columbia's flight deck shows how many switches and controls are involved in flying a shuttle. A keyboard, linked to five inboard computers, dominates the centre foreground. Three screens at the front provide up-to-date flight information.

Commander John Young (left) and pilot Robert Crippen run through check-lists during a rehearsal for their first space shuttle mission on Columbia. Pilot astronauts train for up to 25 hours a week, for 11 weeks, on a shuttle mission simulator.

Reaching for the stars

Shuttle crews normally consist of a flight commander, a pilot and three specialists who are usually scientists. Only the commander and pilot have to be able to fly the shuttle, but all the astronauts have to go through a tough training programme. They need to be physically fit. One of their first challenges is to learn how to live without gravity – absolutely everything is weightless in space. It is a topsy-turvy world where it's impossible to walk like we do on Earth. (Astronauts say it's great fun to float anywhere they like.) As well as using the space flight simulators described on p. 26, there are several other ways in which astronauts here on Earth can experience some of the sensations of being in space. It is possible to get quite close to being completely weightless if you are under water, so it helps if an astronaut knows how to swim.

Left: As part of their training, American astronauts experience brief periods of weightlessness in a specially modified Boeing 707 that climbs skywards and then goes into a steep dive. Not surprisingly, it's been nicknamed the 'vomit comet'!

Astronauts are strapped into a container on the end of an arm that spins around extremely fast. This centrifuge helps them to get used to the feeling of accelerating into space at great speed.

American astronaut Bruce McCandless tests a manned manoeuvring unit (MMU) in the Weightless Environment Training Facility (WET-F) – a deep pool – at the Johnson Space Centre, Houston, Texas.

Soviet cosmonauts train in a huge pool at Star City in Moscow, Russia, for operations that will eventually be carried out for real on the outside of space station Mir. A huge mock-up of Mir is submerged 5 m (16 ft) down and cosmonauts in specially modified spacesuits carry out 'repairs' or other mission tasks in what are almost perfect weightless conditions.

Space walks outside Mir are becoming more and more commonplace so this type of training is extremely important. Cosmonauts learn what it is like to move around in space, and what it is like to work there. In the safety of a swimming pool, here on Planet Earth, they can rehearse, and rehearse again, what might be an extremely complicated and dangerous task in space.

Living in space

A typical shuttle mission lasts for between nine and 10 days and during that time the shuttle is home *and* workplace for the crew. The 'air' in the pressurised flight deck, mid-deck living quarters and Spacelab (when carried) is similar to the air we breathe on Earth: it is composed of 80 per cent nitrogen and 20 per cent oxygen. In these areas the flight crew and mission specialists can wear clothes like jump suits. Their main problem is weightlessness. It affects the way they eat, sleep, work and even go to the lavatory.

Mid-deck
This is the crew's living quarters – a kitchen, dining-room, lounge, bathroom and bedroom rolled into one.

Flight deck
This contains all the shuttle's control systems. The commander and pilot fly the spacecraft from here.

Food and even liquid can float around in 'blobs', so astronauts have to eat and drink with care. On early missions, choice was limited and food was eaten straight from containers like toothpaste tubes. In fact, most foods *can* be handled with ordinary forks and spoons. Now there is a choice of 90 items, including sausages and scrambled eggs.

Some foods, like biscuits and bread, come in normal form but are moistened to prevent crumbs flying everywhere. Other food comes in tins or flexible packs. It is often dried to save space and is prepared by adding water.

The solar cells that use energy from the sun to make electricity for the shuttle produce hydrogen and this, combined with oxygen, makes water for the crew.

A meal for one on the Soviet Mir space station. Some tubes are used but most food comes in tins or flexible packs.

Lavatory
The shuttle's lavatory is very different from those on Earth. It uses airflow instead of water to get rid of waste.

Airlock
This tunnel allows astronauts to move freely between the mid-deck and Spacelab, which fits neatly into the payload bay.

Spacelab
Scientists can carry out major experiments in Spacelab, which is about the size of a double-decker bus, when it is taken on shuttle missions.

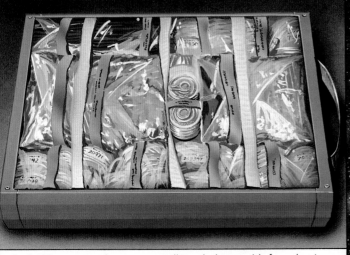

Each US astronaut has a personally coded tray with four days' supply of food. The trays are stored in the mid-deck lockers.

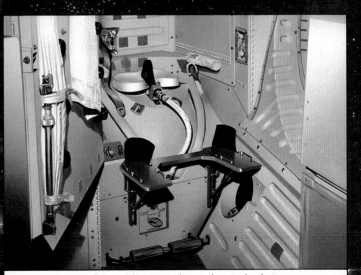

Water doesn't flow without gravity, so lavatories in space use an airflow system to pull waste materials away from the body.

Floating free

To get around in a weightless world, astronauts have to pull or push themselves along ceilings, walls or floors. The only way they can stay still is to grab hold of something and hang on tight. They are living in an environment without gravity – a 'Zero-G' environment – and they can't keep their feet on the ground unless they are strapped down. Everything, including tools and personal belongings, has to be stuck down or it would simply float away.

Despite their training, weightlessness makes it difficult for astronauts to work and carry out experiments. It also makes some space travellers feel ill; about half of all astronauts suffer from 'space sickness' for the first few days of a space flight. People in space look different from the way they look on Earth. This is because more blood than usual goes to the head which makes the face look fatter. Astronauts would also grow taller if they were in space for any great length of time. There is no gravity to keep their bones compacted together.

Regular exercise is extremely important. Muscles are not worked as hard in the weightless conditions of space as they are on Earth, so they can weaken and turn into 'flab'.

There is no 'up' or 'down' in space and astronauts could sleep in any position. But they use sleeping-bags attached to the wall. It stops them banging into each other while sleeping and they can go to sleep knowing they will wake up in the same place.

The crew of the shuttle Columbia enjoy the topsy-turvy world of space.

Astronaut Owen Garriott (left) carries out medical tests on Byron Lichtenberg in Spacelab, aboard the shuttle Columbia.

Having a haircut in the weightless conditions of space is a tricky business and an astronaut has to trust his barber. A 'vacuum cleaner' sucks up loose bits of hair.

Astronaut Gerald Carr performs some weightless gymnastics during the final Skylab mission. It lasted 84 days, from 16 November 1973 until 8 February 1974 – the longest period an American crew has stayed in space.

Keeping fit in space doesn't get astronauts any distance at all – they exercise on treadmills, wearing an elastic harness that holds them down as they row or run on the spot.

SLEEP RESTRAINT

Dr Sally Ride, America's first female astronaut, prepares for bed in a 'sleep restraint' anchored to the wall of the space shuttle Challenger.

Dressing up

Astronauts can breathe easily and can wear casual clothes in the pressurised sections of a spacecraft. This is because Earth-like living conditions have been re-created. But space is hostile – there is no air and it is scorching hot in the sun and freezing cold in the shade. There is also danger from radiation or from tiny fragments of rock, called meteoroids. Outside the craft, astronauts wear specially designed spacesuits that make them look more like aliens than human beings.

The suits, made with several layers of different materials, come in two main parts: a hard upper half and a more flexible lower half. The two sections, white to reflect the sun's harmful rays, simply snap together. Underneath, the astronaut wears a 'cooling' suit, complete with a network of narrow tubes of circulating water that stops the body overheating.

Manned manoeuvring unit (MMU)
The astronaut moves around on an MMU powered by tiny gas jets.

Spacesuit (lower half)
The bottom half is flexible and, like the rest of the suit, is made with several layers of material which protect the astronaut and keep his or her body at the right pressure.

American Bruce McCandless makes the first untethered space walk. He travelled 90 m (300 ft) from Challenger on 7 November 1984 with the help of a manned manoeuvring unit (see top right).

TV camera
An automatic, battery-powered video camera can feed 'live' pictures to Earth via the spacecraft.

Helmet and visor
A separate helmet, with darkened visor, provides protection from the sun. Underneath, the astronaut wears a special cap with built-in microphone and headphone so that he can communicate with the spacecraft.

Portable life support system (PLSS)
A pack, attached to the back of the spacesuit, contains enough water and oxygen for the astronaut to survive for seven hours outside the spacecraft.

Spacesuit (upper half)
The hard top half is lined with an aluminium shell for protection.

Notepad
A pad contains mission briefing notes.

Gloves
Special gloves, multi-layered like the spacesuit, allow maximum finger movement.

MMU controls
The MMU is controlled by joysticks on panels.

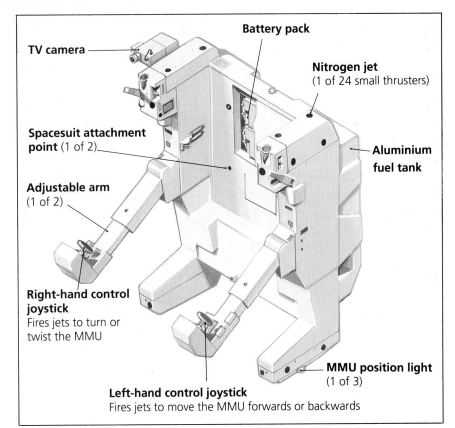

TV camera

Battery pack

Nitrogen jet
(1 of 24 small thrusters)

Spacesuit attachment point (1 of 2)

Aluminium fuel tank

Adjustable arm
(1 of 2)

Right-hand control joystick
Fires jets to turn or twist the MMU

MMU position light
(1 of 3)

Left-hand control joystick
Fires jets to move the MMU forwards or backwards

Above: The manned manoeuvring unit (MMU) is propelled by 24 small nitrogen gas jets, which can be fired at different times to move the astronaut in any direction. Only three MMUs have been built. Each one cost about $9 million.

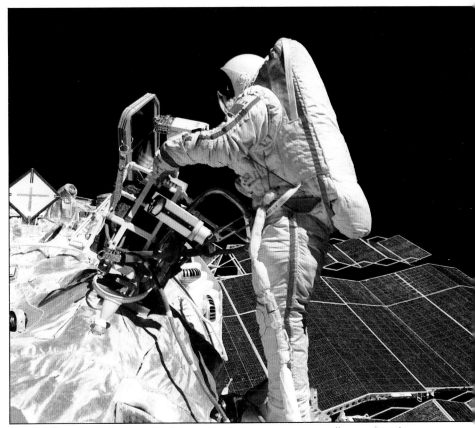

Above: Cosmonaut Svetlana Savitskaya, the first woman space-walker on 25 July 1984. Soviet spacesuits are similar to those used by American astronauts.

Space stations

SCIENTISTS in the USA and the Soviet Union were keen to carry out experiments in space and find out how long people could stay there. So engineers from both countries designed orbiting laboratories that could be visited by manned capsules. They used solar panels so that these space stations would be powered by the sun.

The Soviet Union launched Salyut 1 in 1971. Two years later, in May 1973, the Americans launched their one and only space station: Skylab.

Laboratory in space

Skylab got off to a bad start. A shield to protect the space station against meteoroids tore off, and one of the solar panels jammed. Luckily, astronauts were able to fix these problems. They were the first space travellers to enjoy the earthly creature comforts that Skylab was able to provide: a shower and lavatory and more room to move around in. The last mission was in February 1974, but Skylab remained in orbit until July 1979.

Three crews of three people visited Skylab during its working life. They carried out hundreds of experiments, including many on their own bodies. Between them, they proved that people could stay in space for months at a time without causing serious harm to themselves.

Apollo spacecraft This ferried astronauts to Skylab and then took them safely back to Earth.

Multiple docking adapter This is equipped with two docking ports, one for the command module and a spare in case of an emergency rescue mission.

BEAN GARRIOTT LOUSMA

SKYLAB II

It doesn't look quite right does it? The newly launched Skylab is missing a solar panel that jammed when the gold-coloured meteoroid shield tore off. These faults could have wrecked the entire project, but astronauts sorted out the problems.

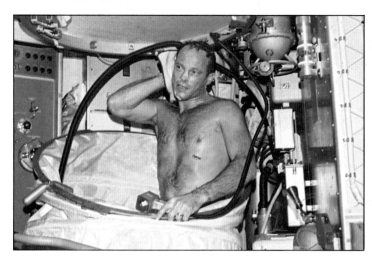

Skylab's shower was the ultimate earthly luxury for space-weary astronauts. A 'vacuum cleaner' sucked up drops of water that went astray.

A record-breaker in its time, Skylab played host to three crews who set new records for the length of time humans spent in space. It orbited the Earth nearly 35,000 times, travelled more than 1.5 billion kilometres and stayed in space for 2249 days.

Solar panels These X-shaped panels trapped the sun's rays and transformed them into electricity to power the equipment on Skylab.

Solar panel This panel jammed as it unfolded during Skylab's launch (see photograph left).

Telescope mount Telescopes were placed here, outside the craft, to study the sun.

Airlock module Astronauts had to pass through this module before going for a space walk.

Oxygen tanks

Water tanks

Bedroom (or 'sleep compartment')

Waste collection

Porthole

Freezer For storing space meals.

Shower One of the comforts of home, it made long stays in space more bearable . . . and cleaner!

Orbital workshop The lower level provided living space for the crew; the upper level was for storage and equipment.

'Hotel' in orbit

The Soviet Union had launched seven Salyut space stations, each one better than the last, before launching a new model, Mir (the Russian word for 'peace'), in 1986. Since then Mir has been visited by numerous cosmonauts. Two of them, Vladimir Titov and Musa Manarov, stayed for a whole year. It is designed as the heart of a much bigger, permanent, space complex and has six docking ports where new sections can be added on. Two Kvant modules and the Kristall module already in place provide extra equipment and more room.

Mir gets its power from the sun, although it uses liquid fuel when it needs an extra boost – for instance, in order to move into a new position. The cosmonauts spend most of their working hours in the spacecraft/ laboratory in which they travelled to Mir. They relax in the 'core' station, which is a laboratory in its own right. Unmanned Progress cargocraft provide a taxi service from Earth to Mir, bringing fresh supplies of food and water, and even letters from home. The cosmonauts reload Progress with their rubbish and send it back to Earth.

'Core' station Contains basic scientific equipment and was launched in 1986. Mir was designed so that new parts could be added on using the six docking ports.

Solar panels

This photograph of Mir was taken in 1988 and shows Kvant 1, the first module to be added after the 'core' station was launched in 1986. Others have since been connected. Now there are plans for a Mir 2.

МИР

The interior of Mir, the orbiting space hotel. It is a comfortable place to stay, where visiting cosmonauts can relax after a hard space-day's work. Guests enjoy privacy in separate bedrooms, and there's a washroom and lavatories, a dining-room, and exercise equipment to keep them fit.

Kvant 1 experiment module Launched in 1987. It was the first permanent addition to the 'core' station. It is in two parts. This one is equipped with specialised telescopes to study space.

Kvant 1 service module It backs up the experiment module and is powered by its own solar panels.

Soyuz TM Visiting spacecraft carries a fresh crew of cosmonauts. It is in three parts, with its own service module, an orbital module which navigates the docking with Mir and a descent module that takes the returning crew back to Earth.

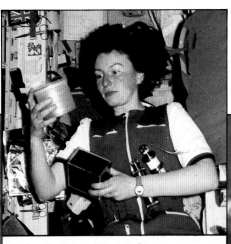

Helen Sharman, Britain's first cosmonaut, finds out what it is really like to have your hair standing on end! She is checking some equipment during her visit to Mir in May 1991.

Leonid Kizim tries to grab a mischievous piece of equipment. He and Vladimir Solovyov were the first cosmonauts to work on board space station Mir when it was launched in 1986.

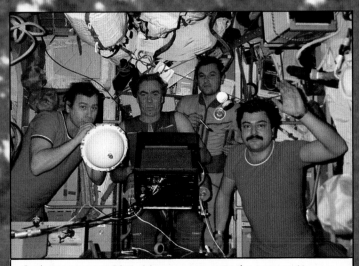

Soviet cosmonaut Musa Manorov waves to the camera. He was embarking on a record-breaking year in space with the cosmonaut next to him, Vladimir Titov.

Space science

INSTRUMENTS on spacecraft are able to carry out a whole range of experiments, all to help us in our endless quest for knowledge. Every voyage is a fresh chance to find out something new about how we could cope with living in space. And, of course, there is always the chance of a discovery that could make life better on Earth.

Below: Future space travel depends on vital experiments on the human body. So, during every mission to space, astronauts carry out medical tests – they use each other as guinea-pigs. Sometimes the astronauts are trained medical doctors.

Right: A camera fixed behind the nose of the shuttle Columbia captures the view back along the craft. The open doors reveal the European-built Spacelab nestling in the cargo bay. Spacelab is ESA's contribution to the American shuttle programme.

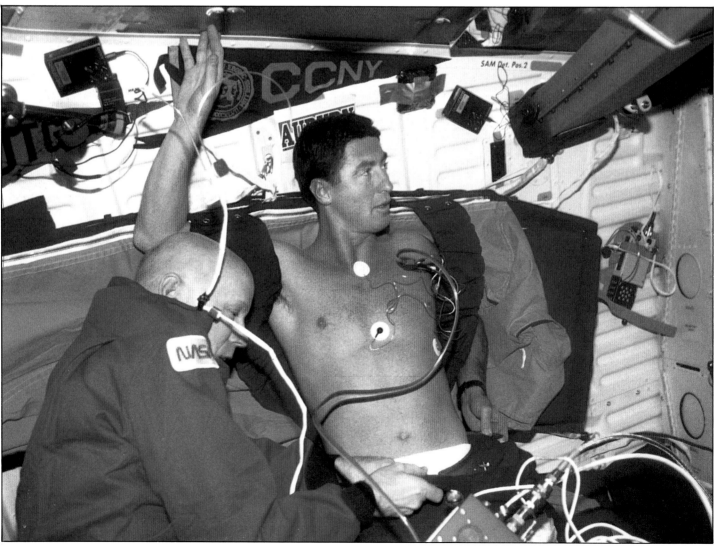

Vital experiments

Why does space travel make so many astronauts sick? Why do they suffer from back-ache? Why do their bones begin to lose calcium, a vital mineral? To help space doctors find the answers, astronauts become guinea-pigs for vital experiments on the human body. They are wired up so that heartbeat, body temperature and blood pressure can be monitored. Their eyes and ears are tested, too.

Other experiments are best carried out when there are no people around. They are designed for a perfectly still environment and if an astronaut caused even a slight disturbance a test could be wrecked. That is why there are plans for unmanned space laboratories. Of course, many experiments depend on astronauts setting them up and checking them at regular intervals.

Above: Arabella the spider successfully spun a web in space in an experiment set by an American schoolgirl, Judith Miles.

Animal, vegetable, mineral

Human beings are not the only creatures that travel to space. Others range from rats to spiders and flies, jellyfish, frogs and monkeys. The effect weightlessness has on them reveals a great deal about what it does to humans.

If there are to be space farms to support human colonies, scientists need to know how plants grow in weightless conditions. It would also be useful to know what building materials could be made in space and used to construct colonies.

Left: To find out how gravity affects plant growth, these mung bean seedlings were germinated in a mini-greenhouse in space. A few stray roots are growing up instead of down.

Above: Astronaut Tamara Jernigan gets to grips with an experiment in a specially sealed unit in Spacelab. She slips her hands into built-in gloves to perform a delicate operation.

Left: Crystals have been known to grow a thousand times bigger in space than they do on Earth. Discoveries of this kind could lead to new commercial industries in space.

Calling the world

IT is easy to forget just how much the conquest of space has transformed our lives back on Planet Earth. Every time we watch a television news report or football match beamed live from another continent, or telephone a friend who lives on the other side of the world, we are making use of satellites orbiting the Earth thousands of kilometres above us.

Satellites are blasted into orbit on board rockets or the space shuttle. Around 400 are in operation at the moment, and they come in all shapes and sizes: unlike rockets or aeroplanes there is no need for them to be streamlined as they have no air to cut through while hurtling round the planet.

They carry out a vast range of jobs, from helping ships find their way across the oceans to collecting vital information about the damage humans are doing to the environment.

Energy from the sun

All satellites need power to operate, and this is usually provided by solar cells which change sunlight into electricity. Satellites like Astra have huge solar panels like wings stretching up to 20 m (60 ft) from tip to tip. Others, like Meteosat, have their solar cells wrapped around them. Much of the power generated is used to increase the strength of weak signals reaching the satellite, before sending them on the long journey back to Earth.

Breakthrough

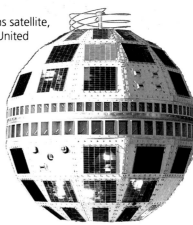

The world's first communications satellite, Telstar 1, was launched by the United States in 1962 and amazed the world by relaying live television pictures from America to Europe. It could also handle 600 telephone calls at a time. The latest satellites can each handle more than 30,000 calls simultaneously.

Television

Astra is used to broadcast the satellite television station BSkyB direct to homes across Western Europe. To receive the signal each house needs a small dish pointing at the satellite – which is around 36,000 km (22,000 miles) away!

Boats and planes

Inmarsat satellites allow telephone calls to be made from boats and aircraft, and also from ship to shore.

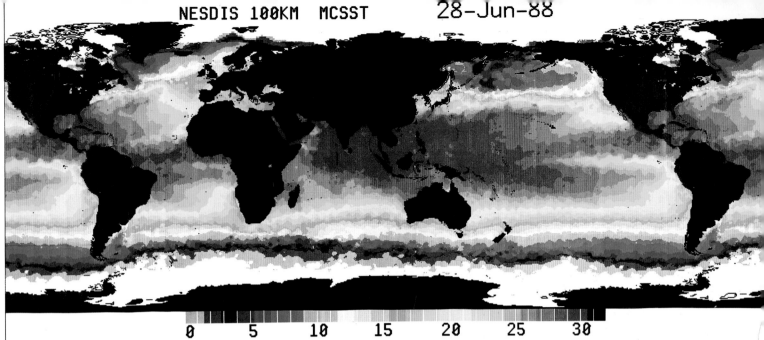

NESDIS 100KM MCSST   28-Jun-88

0   5   10   15   20   25   30
SEA SURFACE TEMPERATURES   DEG C

This map of sea temperature was compiled from readings taken by satellite. It's useful to weather forecasters – and to fishermen, as different fish are found in warmer and cooler waters.

Earthwatch
Landsat 1, launched in 1972, was one of the first satellites to take detailed pictures of the Earth, revealing, for example, whether crops were healthy and even helping to find oil beneath the Earth's surface.

Weather forecasts
Meteosat is Europe's main weather satellite, providing the detailed pictures we see on television forecasts.
(The globe in the centre of this page is a photograph taken by Meteosat.)

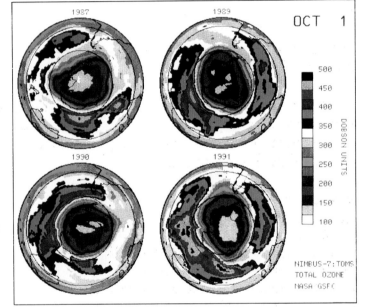

1987   1989   OCT 1

1990   1991

500
450
400
350
300
250
200
150
100

DOBSON UNITS

NIMBUS-7 : TOMS
TOTAL OZONE
NASA GSFC

The alarming discovery that there is a large hole in the Earth's protective ozone layer was made in 1987 using an environmental satellite called Nimbus 7. The hole was found over the Antarctic, and is shown by pink and dark brown areas in the diagrams. It has remained roughly the same size since 1987.

'Standing still' in space
Many communications and weather satellites are sent up to a special orbit 36,000 km (22,000 miles) above the Equator. Here they take exactly a day to complete one orbit of the Earth. And since the planet also takes exactly a day to make one turn, the satellites will always stay above the same point, appearing to be stationary. This 'geostationary' orbit means, for instance, that television satellite dishes receiving pictures from the Astra satellite can always point in the same direction.

Eyes in the sky

Satellite telescopes have revolutionised astronomy, improving our 'view' of the universe dramatically as they don't have to peer through the Earth's murky atmosphere.

In 1990, the huge Hubble space telescope was launched by the space shuttle. It was designed to see seven times further into space than ever before. However, problems with its giant mirror mean it is not yet working quite as well as expected.

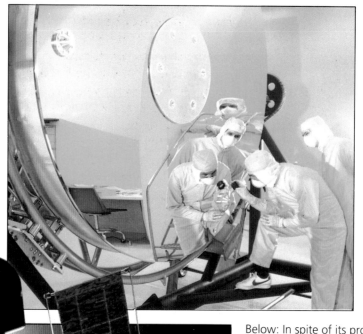

Left: Scientists examine Hubble's huge main mirror before launch. It measures 2½ m (8 ft) across and weighs nearly a tonne. Unfortunately it was made very slightly the wrong shape, so it doesn't focus properly. This wasn't noticed till it was tested in space!

Below: In spite of its problems Hubble still shows a vast improvement over other telescopes, as can be seen by these two images of the same cluster of stars.

An artist's impression of Hubble in space soon after its release from the shuttle's cargo bay.

Computer image produced by a telescope based on Earth.

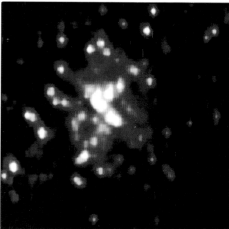

Computer image produced by the Hubble space telescope.

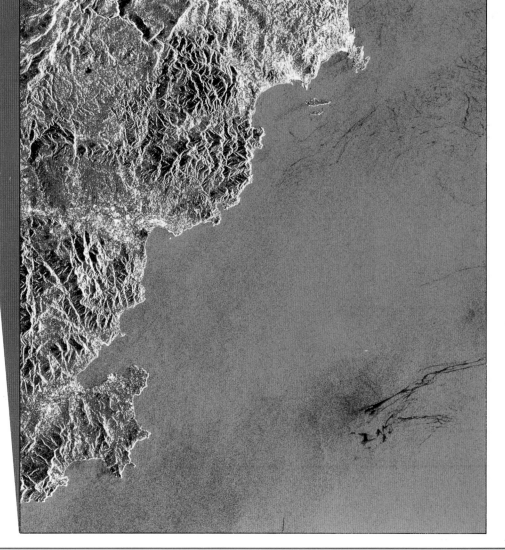

Environment check!

ERS-1 is one of the world's most advanced satellites. It was launched in 1991 by the European Space Agency in response to growing concern about the state of the environment.

Using ERS-1 scientists will for the first time be able to keep a close check on the exact size of the polar ice-caps. If they find the caps are shrinking it will be strong evidence that the world is heating up as a result of pollution in the atmosphere (the so-called greenhouse effect).

Other instruments on ERS-1 measure with incredible accuracy the strength of the wind, the temperature of the sea and the height of the waves.

This ERS-1 image of the south coast of France was taken in September 1991. It gave the first warning that a huge oil slick (bottom right) was threatening French holiday beaches.

Space junk

More than 4000 satellites have been launched over the past 30 years. Most operate for only about 10 years, after which they join the ever-growing heap of space junk circling the planet. Some fall slowly back to Earth, burning up harmlessly in the atmosphere, but others will remain in orbit for thousands of years. Along with old rocket boosters and pieces of debris from more than 100 explosions in space, they pose an increasing threat of collision to spacecraft. There are now urgent calls for international action to find ways to limit space junk.

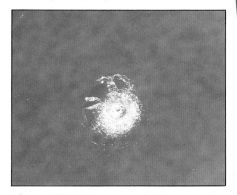

Above: This pit in a space shuttle windscreen was caused by a tiny flake of paint hitting the craft at around 32,000 km (20,000 miles) per hour.

War and space

IT is thought that around two-thirds of the satellites sent into space are military. Modern armies would find it almost impossible to win major wars without their help. 'Spy-in-the-sky' satellites locate enemy targets and monitor troop movements: the best are now believed to be able to see objects as small as 10 cm (4 in.) across from an orbit 160 km (100 miles) above the Earth.

Communications satellites allow commanders to speak directly to their forces on the battlefront, and early-warning satellites spot enemy missiles within seconds of their being launched.

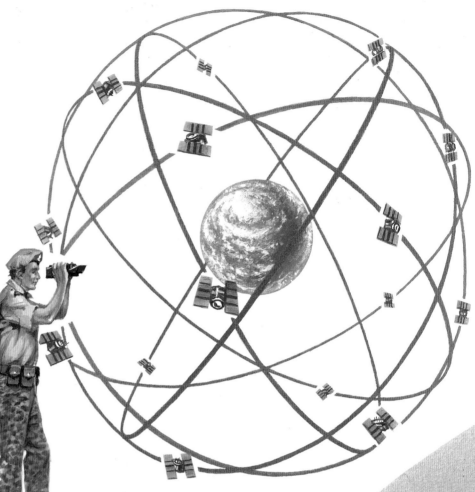

Above: America's 'Global Positioning System' was used to great effect in the Gulf War in 1991. Fifteen satellites circling the Earth enabled soldiers to find out their exact position in the desert using only a small hand-held receiver.

This dramatic satellite picture taken during the Gulf War in 1991 shows oil wells around Kuwait City burning out of control.

4. Interception
Up to 5000 'Brilliant Pebbles' interceptors circle the Earth, waiting for the signal to attack enemy missiles by crashing into them at great speed.

5. Final detection
Another satellite relays information about any surviving missiles to controllers on the ground.

The space shield
This diagram shows some of the possible ways 'Star Wars' might destroy nuclear missiles launched in an attack on America from the East. The system will cost billions of dollars, and its designers hope parts of it will operate by the turn of the century.

'Star Wars'

The Strategic Defense Initiative (SDI) was launched in 1983 by the President of the United States, Ronald Reagan. The project was soon nicknamed 'Star Wars'. It aimed to develop a complete space 'shield' against nuclear attacks, searching out and destroying thousands of long-range missiles in flight. Most scientists now accept that the ambitious project will never provide the total protection dreamt of by President Reagan.

Laser power: a rocket is destroyed by a laser weapon during a test in America.

2. Laser destruction
As the missiles reach the borders of space a powerful laser destroys as many as possible.

1. Early warning
An early-warning satellite detects enemy missiles being launched by sensing the intense heat given out during blast-off.

3. 'Brilliant Eyes'
A 'Brilliant Eyes' satellite tracks remaining missiles and passes on their position to 'Brilliant Pebbles' interceptors.

6. The final defence
'Anti-missile' missiles launched from the Earth's surface provide a final line of defence.

The robot explorers

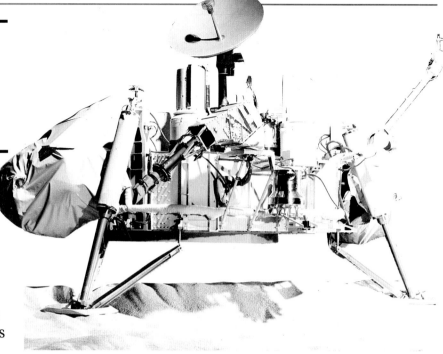

WHILE manned missions have grabbed most of the headlines during the Space Age, unmanned space probes have taught us far more about the solar system. Probes have flown past every planet except Pluto, and have landed on the surface of Earth's two nearest neighbours: Venus and Mars. To begin their long journeys of exploration, probes first have to escape completely from the pull of Earth's gravity. To do this they must be blasted out of Earth orbit at an 'escape velocity' of at least 40,000 km (25,000 miles) per hour. Even at this great speed they take several years to reach the more distant planets. Probes can carry only enough fuel on their journey to make small course corrections. They simply coast through space at a constant speed as there is no air to slow them down.

Above: This is one of two identical Viking probes that were sent to Mars in 1975 to land on the surface and search for life. (Scientists often send two probes in case one fails.) Before the probes set off they were sterilised to make sure no Earth creatures were carried to the 'Red Planet' and mistaken for Martian life forms.

Above: This detailed picture of Mars was taken from orbit. The Viking probes reached the planet after journeys of almost a year. They then parachuted down through the atmosphere, firing retro-rockets for the last few seconds to ensure a smooth landing.

Left: A sensational view of the surface of Mars photographed by Viking. Weather instruments on the probe detected a pleasant light breeze, but freezing temperatures as low as – 80°C (–112°F). Viking's automatic laboratory carried out several experiments on soil samples but found no signs of life.

Below: Venus is completely covered by thick cloud, so it is impossible to get an overall picture of the planet using telescopes. The Magellan probe arrived in orbit in 1990, and is using an advanced radar to 'peer through' the clouds and map the planet's surface.

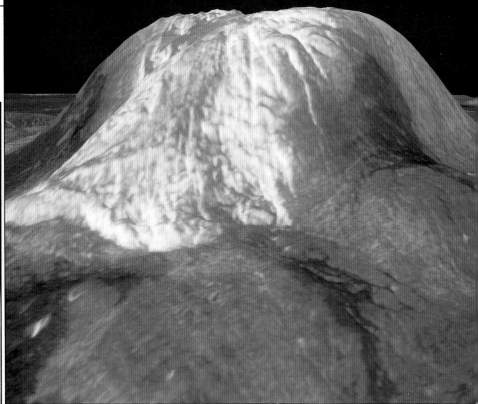

Above: Magellan scans the entire surface of Venus strip by strip from an orbit about 300 km (200 miles) above the planet. Computers back on Earth then analyse the results to produce exceptionally detailed images of the mountainous Venusian landscape.

Probing the planets

		First fly-past	First successful landing
Sun			
Mercury		Mariner 10, 1974	
Venus		Mariner 2, 1962	Venera 9, 1975
Earth			
Moon		Luna 3, 1959	Luna 9, 1966
Mars		Mariner 4, 1965	Viking 1, 1976
Jupiter		Pioneer 10, 1973	
Saturn		Pioneer 11, 1979	
Uranus		Voyager 2, 1986	
Neptune		Voyager 2, 1989	
Pluto			

Halley's comet
Halley's comet (below) has fascinated people throughout history, streaking past the Earth every 76 years. When it returned in 1986, the European Space Agency's Giotto probe (bottom) flew into the comet to take the first-ever close-up picture (inset).

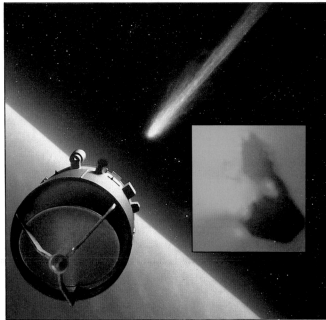

Voyagers' travels

The epic voyages of Voyager 1 and Voyager 2 were an extra-ordinary success, sending back spectacular pictures of all the outer planets except Pluto.

Voyager 2's 12-year journey over billions of kilometres relied on an event which happens only once every few hundred years. Around 1980 Jupiter, Saturn, Uranus and Neptune were lined up in such a way that as Voyager 2 flew past each one in turn, each planet's gravity acted like a sling speeding the probe to its next encounter.

By the time Voyager 2 reached Neptune, the information radioed back by the probe at the speed of light was taking more than four hours to reach us. (Radio signals from the moon take less than 1½ seconds to travel to Earth.) Scientists had to use great ingenuity to turn the incredibly faint radio signals into the stunning full-colour pictures on the right.

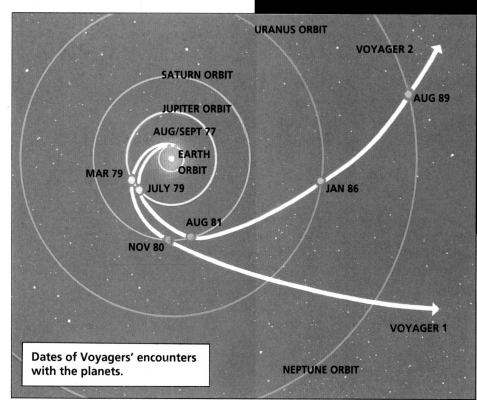

Dates of Voyagers' encounters with the planets.

Jupiter
Voyagers 1 and 2 photographed not only the giant planet itself, but also its four main moons. The probes revealed that the famous Great Red Spot on Jupiter is made up of storm clouds that whirl round with unbelievable ferocity.

Saturn
Dramatic pictures of Saturn taken by both probes showed that the three rings seen from

MOONS OF JUPITER

SATURN

NEPTUNE

JUPITER

VOYAGER

URANUS

MIRANDA (MOON OF URANUS)

Earth are in fact made up of thousands of thinner rings.

After flying past Saturn, Voyager 1 headed away to take measurements of the solar wind (electrical particles given out by the sun).

Uranus
Voyager 2 was now in uncharted territory 3 billion km (2 billion miles) from Earth. No space probe had flown past Uranus or Neptune before. Voyager could make out no features on the surface of Uranus, but its photograph of one of the five known moons showed some weird grooves and ridges. The probe also discovered 10 more moons orbiting the bluish-green planet.

Neptune
After a 12-year journey covering around 6 billion km (4 billion miles), Voyager 2 had its closest encounter of all. The probe sped past Neptune just 5000 km (3000 miles) above its cloudy surface. It measured wind speeds of 2000 km (1300 miles) per hour on the surface, the strongest ever found in the solar system, and discovered six new moons bringing the planet's known total to eight.

Following its encounter with Neptune, Voyager 2 headed out of the solar system and is now on an endless journey into deep space. It carries objects designed to tell any alien beings that may exist that there is life on Earth (see p. 75).

Mission control

EVERY mission to space is controlled from the ground. If the spacecraft is launching satellites, their progress is often monitored at a different control room from that of the spacecraft itself.

When an American shuttle is being prepared for blast-off, the Kennedy Space Centre at the launch site at Cape Canaveral in Florida controls the countdown and launch. But once the shuttle has left the ground, the Johnson Space Centre in Houston, Texas, takes over, keeping control of the shuttle and its crew. Everything the astronauts do in space is checked with Mission Control there, which operates round-the-clock.

FOD
Flight Operations
Directorate.

Flight director
Call sign 'Flight'. In charge of the team and makes all the decisions about the mission.

World map
Shows the path of the orbiting shuttle.

Guidance officer
Call sign 'Guidance'. Monitors navigation of the shuttle by the crew and on-board computers.

Spacecraft communicator
Call sign 'Capcom'. Talks to the shuttle crew, relaying information and messages from the flight control team.

Astronaut Sally Ride keeps in close touch with Mission Control, to make sure everything is going according to plan. There are slight delays in the conversation just as there are with a long-distance telephone call.

Mission Control, Johnson Space Centre, Houston, Texas, is in charge of all American manned space flights once the rockets have left the launch pad at Cape Canaveral. The team use 'call signs' and not their normal names when they speak to each other. Each work station is labelled according to the job that is done there.

SSPO/OPO

TV screen
Shows live pictures beamed back to Earth from space.

Data processing systems engineer
Studies the information provided by the shuttle's on-board computers.

Monitoring positions
SSPO stands for Space Shuttle Program Office and OPO is the Orbiter Project Office.

Flight activities officer
Plans the crew's activities.

Data screen
This is packed with facts and figures relating to the mission.

Disasters

ALL stages of a space flight carry great dangers. At blast-off astronauts are sitting just above a massive controlled explosion and once in orbit any damage to the craft may result in all air being lost to the vacuum of space. The United States and the Soviet Union have each flown over 70 missions, and to date each has had two fatal accidents. Worst of all was the American Challenger disaster of 1986. To the world it had seemed like just another routine shuttle launch, the 25th in less than five years. Then 73 seconds after blast-off Challenger exploded, killing all seven astronauts on board. It was later found that one of the rocket boosters had developed a leak. Flights started again 2½ years later – but it will be a long time before anybody again takes space travel for granted.

Christa McAuliffe, one of the astronauts who died aboard Challenger, was to have been the first teacher in space, carrying out experiments suggested by children and conducting live lessons with schools back on Earth. An 'apple for the teacher' was included in the design of the mission space patch (below) to mark the event.

Above: This photograph of Challenger taken at lift-off shows black smoke (ringed) beginning to leak from the rocket booster.

The three Apollo 1 astronauts died in 1967 in a tragic accident a month before their flight was due to blast off. A spark set off a fire in their cabin as the craft sat on the launch pad during a routine test.

SOVIET DISASTERS

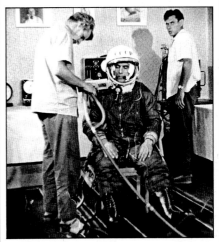

Vladimir Komarov, seen here in training, was the first man to be killed during a spaceflight. He died in 1967 when the parachute of his Soyuz 1 got tangled, and the spacecraft plunged to the ground.

In 1971 the three-man crew of Soyuz 11 also died in the final stages of their mission. A valve failed during re-entry and all the air in the craft rushed out.

Seconds after the American shuttle Challenger exploded off the coast of Florida, wreckage can be seen plummeting towards the sea.

Space rescue

'HOUSTON, we've had a problem . . .' Those words calmly radioed back to Mission Control by Apollo 13 astronaut Jack Swigert signalled the start of the greatest real-life space rescue the world has seen.

The Apollo 13 mission was due to make the third manned landing on the moon in April 1970. People superstitious about the number 13 had particular reason for concern as the mission blasted off at 13:13 Houston time! And two days later, as Apollo 13 approached the moon, the date was . . . 13 April! Suddenly there was a loud bang and the whole craft shuddered. An oxygen tank had exploded in the service module.

As the three astronauts in the command module urgently tried to work out what had happened, they noticed their oxygen and electricity levels falling rapidly. Out of the window they could see gas pouring into space.

Their situation was critical, 320,000 km (200,000 miles) from Earth. Frantically, mission controllers back in Houston hatched a desperate rescue plan. The only hope was to abandon the moon landing and instead use the lunar module as a 'lifeboat' for the crew. With just a few minutes of oxygen remaining in the command module, the astronauts crawled through to the lunar module cabin.

But their troubles were far from over. The lunar module only had enough power supplies for one day, half the time needed for the journey home. The crew could survive only by cutting back drastically on heat and light. As the temperature in the cabin fell to 3°C (37°F) and frost began to form on the inside of the windows, the tired astronauts had to make critical course corrections to steer the craft round the moon and back to Earth.

Twice they made heart-stopping mistakes as they became more and more exhausted, but they kept their nerve and returned home safely to a heroes' welcome.

Apollo 13 astronauts Jack Swigert, Jim Lovell and Fred Haise demonstrate a model of their spacecraft during preparations for the ill-fated mission.

Service module Designed to supply the command module with oxygen, electricity and water. The explosion tore a huge hole in its side.

Lunar module Normally used by two astronauts to descend to the surface of the moon. Instead it acted as a 'lifeboat' for the three-man Apollo 13 crew.

The exhausted crew caught their first glimpse of the severely damaged service module as they ditched it a few hours before re-entry. This view shows how a lower panel was blown away by the explosion.

Command module The usual 'home' of the Apollo astronauts. After the explosion, the crew had to abandon it and crawl through to the lunar module.

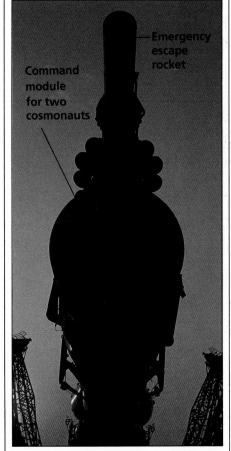

Emergency escape rocket

Command module for two cosmonauts

The Soviet emergency abort system saved the lives of two cosmonauts in 1983 when their rocket caught fire on the launch pad. A smaller escape rocket at the top of the main launcher pulled their command module clear of the blazing wreckage.

As they approached the Earth, the crew put on spacesuits (with emergency oxygen supplies) and crawled into the command module. The lunar module could not withstand re-entry into our atmosphere.

Finally the lunar 'lifeboat' was ditched, and the astronauts plummeted back to Earth in the command module, landing safely in the Pacific Ocean. They had won their race against time.

All in a day's work

WITH satellites costing up to $200 million each to build and launch, rescuing and repairing them is big business. The American space shuttle first repaired a satellite in orbit in a historic mission in April 1984.

The Solar Max satellite had failed just nine months into its expected 10-year life when some of its fuses blew. Shuttle mission 11 aimed to capture Solar Max and bring it into the shuttle cargo bay for repair. For the first time, the astronauts would be able to make use of the manned manoeuvring unit (MMU) which had been tested during the previous shuttle flight.

Astronaut George Nelson steered the MMU perfectly to the crippled satellite, only to find a faulty docking device prevented him from latching on to it! Two days later a new plan to pull Solar Max aboard using the shuttle's robot arm met with complete success. Within hours, the satellite was fully repaired and back in Earth orbit.

Astronaut George Nelson is dwarfed by the huge Solar Max satellite as he attempts in vain to dock with it using the MMU.

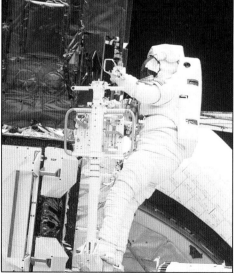

Solar Max is repaired in the space shuttle's cargo bay. The astronaut's feet are held in restraints to stop him floating away.

Right: The MMU was successfully used during shuttle mission 14 in November 1984 to capture two faulty satellites: the Westar 6 and Palapa B2. Here astronaut Dale Gardner is using the MMU to make his final approach to the Westar 6 satellite.

The faulty satellite Intelsat 6 is dragged aboard the shuttle Endeavour by hand in a record-breaking three-man space walk (14 May 1992).

Eurospace

WHILE the United States and the Soviet Union were making huge strides in space travel in the 1960s, several countries in Europe were struggling to make their mark. But exploring space is an expensive business and they realised it made better sense to pool their resources and work together. France had begun building a space centre in French Guiana in South America. This became the launch site for joint European missions.

The European Space Agency (ESA) was born in 1974, and the first Ariane rocket was launched in 1979. The agency has built up a successful business renting out rocket space to anyone – including the Americans – who wants to launch a satellite. In addition, ESA has built research satellites like ERS-1 (see p. 45) and the space probe Giotto, which went to study Halley's comet in 1986. It also built the Spacelab module, which fits into the United States space shuttle for scientific experiments and was first launched in 1983.

FRENCH GUIANA

Europe's space port is in Kourou, French Guiana, on the edge of the South American rainforest. It is just about the best launch site in the world. It's next to the sea, so if a rocket develops a problem and comes shooting back to Earth it is less likely to harm people and the environment. And good weather conditions mean the launch timetable doesn't get wrecked.

Launch tower Stationary tower 12 m (39 ft) from the rocket. It is also called the 'umbilical tower' because of the pipes and cables that connect it to the rocket.

Ariane 4 The rocket's cargo is safely stored in the payload bay in its nose.

Fuel storage

Mission Control Looks after the progress of the launch vehicle, monitors the countdown and is responsible for last-minute checks. Once the rocket has been launched the satellites' progress is monitored from another control room a few miles away.

Launch pad Reinforced platform that anchors the rocket to the ground via the mobile support table.

Flame bucket This is dug deep into the ground directly below the rocket to catch flames on blast-off.

Vertical assembly dock The rocket is put together in an upright position here, ready to be rolled out for the launch.

Savannah Natural clearing in the rainforest. Minimum damage was done to the environment when the space centre was built.

Mobile tower Protects the rocket until shortly before launch, when it is rolled back to the position shown here. It is 80 m (262 ft) high and allows access to the space vehicle and its payload.

Ground safety Team from the Paris fire brigade is on stand-by in case of accident. It is equipped with engines, fire extinguishers and ambulances.

Mobile support table Base on which the rocket is moved to launch position.

Rail track Used to roll Ariane out of the assembly area. It takes nearly an hour to move the rocket the 950 m (1000 yds) to the launch pad. The mobile protective tower is then placed over the rocket.

Security Closed circuit television is installed around the space centre. Soldiers patrol the area regularly. 24 hours before launch road-blocks are set up around the launch site to prevent any intrusions.

Rocket power

On Christmas Eve 1979, the European space programme blasted into business. The first Ariane was successfully launched from the jungle space port in Kourou. Customers began queuing up to use the Ariane rockets to put their satellites into orbit.

A family of Arianes grew and, in 1988, the rainforest echoed with the thunder of the first Ariane 4 launch. Bigger and more powerful than any of its predecessors, it made as much noise as 30 Concordes and travelled at almost 30 times the speed of sound.

Since then, Europe's ambitious plans for the future have been fraught with money problems and many projects have been delayed.

Britain has chosen to concentrate on building satellites rather than sending people into space. It is now among the top five countries in satellite technology.

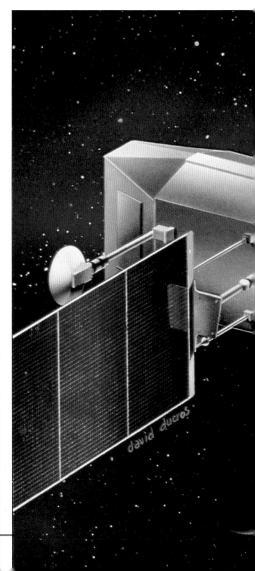

An Ariane 4 blasts into space from its jungle launch pad.

Next step . . .

Ariane 5, due to be launched in 1995, will be Europe's biggest rocket, and will eventually carry people as well as satellites. Astronauts will travel in a shuttle, Hermes, to space station Freedom (see p. 66) and Europe's science laboratories. Hermes is designed to sit on top of the rocket.

Project Columbus

ESA has taken the name of the great European explorer for its most complex space project. The Columbus attached module will be permanently docked on to Freedom, and provide a place for visiting European astronauts to live and work. The Columbus free flyer, a separate science laboratory, will orbit Earth directly behind Freedom. Long-term experiments will be controlled by on-board computers monitored from Earth and checked every six months by visiting astronauts. The Columbus polar platform, a satellite, will travel in a near-polar orbit that takes it in a circle over the north and south poles. It will study Earth's oceans, land and atmosphere.

Right: Ariane 5, Europe's versatile rocket of the future. Unmanned, it will be capable of launching a new generation of bigger, heavier satellites. Or it will carry Hermes and its crew of three to space.

Below: The Columbus free flyer space laboratory. Hermes will dock for short stays while astronauts fix any faults and check that experiments are going to plan.

International space players

THERE are other important players in the space adventure apart from the USA, the USSR and the European Space Agency. Many countries around the world can build their own satellites – they just have to get them launched by somebody else!

Astronauts of several nationalities have travelled in either Soviet or American spacecraft. And a wide variety of experiments have been done in space on behalf of countries that cannot get people there themselves.

Japan

In February 1970, Japan became the fourth nation to launch its own satellite successfully. But so far its space activities have been modest compared to those of America and the Soviet Union. It has two launch sites, both close to the ocean. However, launches are restricted to a few months a year. This is because Japan's fishermen are a very powerful group and they insist that there must be the least possible disturbance to the fish. Nevertheless, Japan has ambitious plans: a re-usable space plane called Hope; a permanent base on the moon; and a module for carrying out experiments, that will fit on to the international space station Freedom (see p. 66).

(see p. 66)

China

China followed close on the heels of Japan and launched its first satellite just two months later. The satellite broadcast a piece of music called 'The East is Red'. The Chinese have long been fascinated by space – they were among the first astronomers.

Today, China sends rockets into space from two launch sites, one in the mountains of central China, one close to the Gobi desert. It has built up a reliable launch service and sells rocket space to countries that want their satellites sent into orbit.

This Japanese rocket carried the Susei space probe, which went into orbit around the sun to get a good look at Halley's comet.

Far left: An unmanned Chinese rocket called 'Long March 3' blasts off without a hitch – its mission to launch a communications satellite into Earth orbit.

Left: Standing in the shadow of China's space technology. This ground station monitors the information sent back to Earth from Chinese orbiting satellites.

India

India started spending money on its space programme when the Soviet Union and America were racing to get the first person into space. But it was another 17 years before a satellite was successfully launched from Indian soil. The country has tried to make its space projects benefit its enormous population, most of whom make a living from the land. So satellites have been launched to monitor the weather for farmers, and to give people television and telephones.

The space age in rural India. The country's first experimental telecommunications satellite undergoes pre-launch tests on the back of a wooden bullock cart. The satellite brought telephones and television to people in outlying districts.

Space travellers from the rest of the world

People from many countries have gone into space. Most of them travelled on Soviet craft to the Salyut or Mir space stations. However, from time to time United States shuttles have carried astronauts who were not Americans.

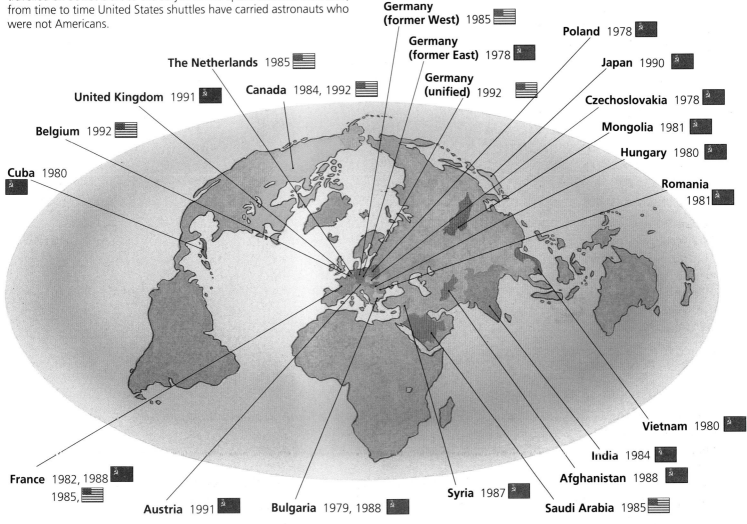

The Netherlands 1985

United Kingdom 1991

Belgium 1992

Cuba 1980

Germany (former West) 1985

Germany (former East) 1978

Germany (unified) 1992

Canada 1984, 1992

Poland 1978

Japan 1990

Czechoslovakia 1978

Mongolia 1981

Hungary 1980

Romania 1981

Vietnam 1980

India 1984

Afghanistan 1988

Saudi Arabia 1985

Syria 1987

Bulgaria 1979, 1988

Austria 1991

France 1982, 1988 1985,

Space station Freedom

IN 1984, America's President Ronald Reagan gave the go-ahead for one of the most exciting and adventurous projects: space station Freedom, the biggest-ever permanently manned orbiting base in space.

The United States is the main partner but Canada, Japan and several countries from the European Space Agency (ESA), including Britain, are also involved. The space station will be a laboratory in space, an environmental observatory and a service station where space planes, including Europe's manned space-craft Hermes (p. 63), can dock and even be repaired. There are also plans for Freedom to have its own fleet of orbital manoeuvring vehicles (OMVs) to recover faulty satellites for repair.

Space station Freedom will also be a launching pad for future missions that will take astronauts back to the moon and beyond.

Facts and figures

The aim is to start building Freedom in 1995 and to complete it by the year 2000. It will be the first 'building' constructed in space and 25 shuttle missions will transport the materials to build it. It will be powered by eight groups of solar panels that will convert sunlight into 75,000 watts of electricity.

An artist's impression of the futuristic space station Freedom. At first, it will have a permanent crew of four, who will stay for three months at a time. But it is hoped that eventually as many as eight astronauts will live on the station for periods of up to six months each.

Destination Mars

ON 20 July 1989, 20 years to the day since man first stepped on to the moon, President Bush of America set a new goal: to land people on Mars by 2019. But whereas it took just a week to fly to the moon and back, a round trip to Mars will last about three years. Food, water and oxygen will either have to be taken from Earth, or generated during the expedition in a special space greenhouse called a 'biosphere'. And nobody knows precisely how people will be affected by such a long period of weightlessness.

The 'Red Planet' is freezing cold, and its thin atmosphere contains no oxygen. As on the moon, astronauts will have to wear spacesuits to walk on the surface. They will stay for several months, until the Earth is in just the right position for a return journey. From their lonely Martian outpost, home will appear as no more than a bright 'star' in the night sky!

An artist's impression of a spacecraft in orbit around Mars. A smaller circular landing craft is shown docked at the far end before its descent to the surface of the planet.

A landing craft fires its retro-rockets to help cushion the impact as it approaches the rocky surface of Mars. It would probably carry enough supplies for astronauts to spend several weeks on the planet.

Back to the future

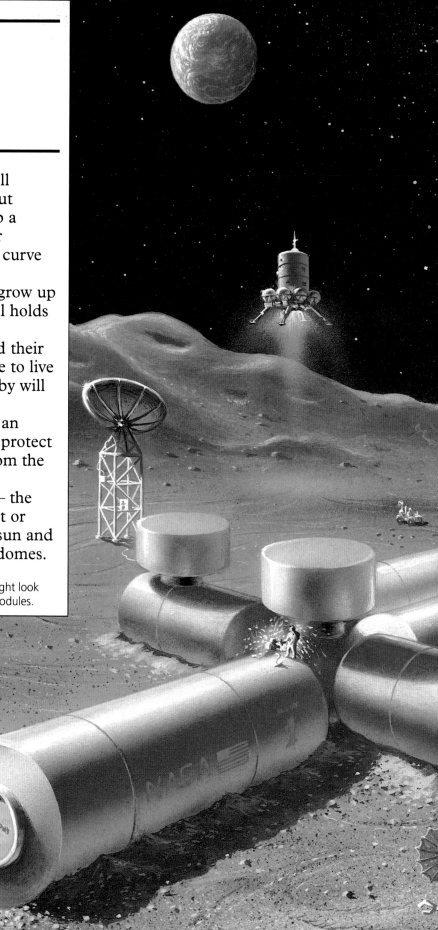

MANY people are convinced we will return to the moon . . . to stay. But before that happens we need to build up a much more detailed picture of the lunar surface, using satellites to map its every curve and crater.

A base on the moon would probably grow up around a mining industry. The lunar soil holds a wealth of riches: iron, titanium and aluminium. Miners, factory workers and their families would be among the first people to live there – some experts believe the first baby will be born on the moon by 2050.

The base in which they live would be an artificial world within a world. It would protect them from cosmic rays and radiation from the sun. And it would provide a controlled environment with an earthly air supply – the moon is airless and can be extremely hot or very cold. Power would come from the sun and vegetables would be grown under food domes.

An idea of what an early permanent base on the moon might look like – a village made from a network of sausage-shaped modules.

Further into the future: a lunar town. Once established, a base would grow into an almost completely self-sufficient community. Within the domes are homes, laboratories and hospitals.

Space cities

WE are polluting our planet in a frightening way and, with the world's population increasing at an alarming rate, the human race may have to look beyond Earth for its survival. Some scientists believe an answer could come in the shape of huge space cities.

The artist's impression on the right shows a city that could house 10,000 people. It is 1600 metres (1 mile) in diameter and its exterior is made from millions of tonnes of lunar rock covered by a protective skin or shell. Space colonists would live in the 'wheel' inside this shell, in landscaped areas with fields, trees and houses, and in an Earth-like environment.

The climate and 'air' would be scientifically controlled so that plants grew efficiently. Careful monitoring of the environment would mean that animals and people in the space cities were healthier than they would be on Planet Earth.

After centuries of dreaming, we finally conquered space. Manned flight and space stations are a reality. But only time will tell whether the vision of huge space cities is a futuristic fantasy or a true insight into a brave new world.

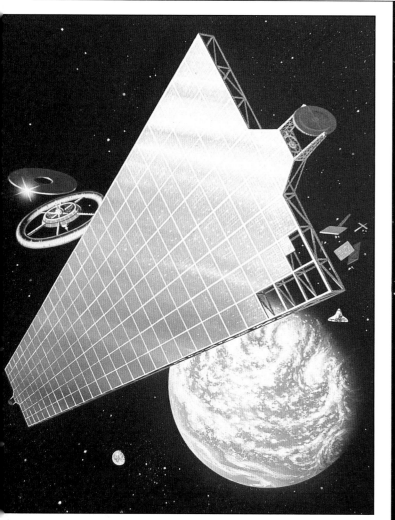

Above: When larger cities are eventually built some of them could include solar-electric power stations like this one, to provide pollution-free electricity for Earth.

Right: This shows the revolving 'wheel' in which people will live. It rotates once a minute. A system of mirrors allows sunlight, but not harmful cosmic radiation, to enter the city.

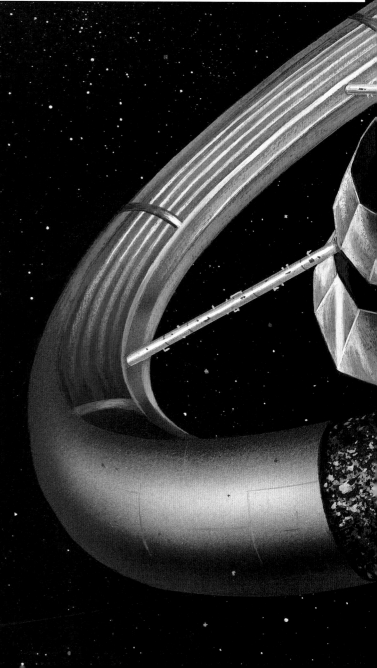

Is anybody out there ?

OUR sun is just one of around 100 billion billion stars in the universe. Many scientists argue that because the universe is so staggeringly huge, it is unlikely that humans are the only intelligent life-form.

Several radio telescopes around the world are taking part in Operation SETI (Search for extraterrestrial intelligence), sending radio signals into deep space and listening out for similar signals being sent to us. Meanwhile, four space probes are currently travelling beyond our solar system: Pioneer 10 and 11, and Voyager 1 and 2 (see p. 50). On board are various objects designed to tell any alien beings about life back on Earth. Voyager 1 is travelling fastest of all at around 64,000 km (40,000 miles) per hour, but will still take thousands of years to reach the nearest star. Even if an alien civilisation exists, it may be too far away for us ever to make contact.

The universe
The Milky Way is itself just one of perhaps a billion galaxies in the universe. Some are spiral-shaped like the Milky Way, others form S-shapes or brilliant discs of colour. Each collection of stars is an unimaginable distance from the next.

Our galaxy
The sun is just one of 100 billion stars in our galaxy, the Milky Way. The stars form a beautiful spiral shape, so huge that even light travelling at 300,000 km (186,000 miles) per second would take 100,000 years to cross it. (Astronomers refer to this as a distance of 100,000 light years.)

Our solar system
It takes present-day spacecraft at least 10 years to travel to the outermost planets Neptune and Pluto, a distance of around 5 billion km (3 million miles). But the whole solar system is a mere speck in the vastness of space.

Another world?

Planets outside our solar system are far too small and faint to see using present-day telescopes like the one on the left. But in 1991 American astronomers made a historic discovery. Their measurements of the movement of a nearby star proved for the first time that there was definitely a planet orbiting round it. The discovery raised hopes that many solar systems in the universe may have planets with similar conditions to those on Earth, allowing them to support life.

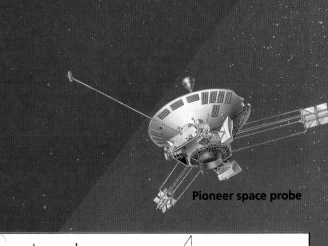

Pioneer space probe

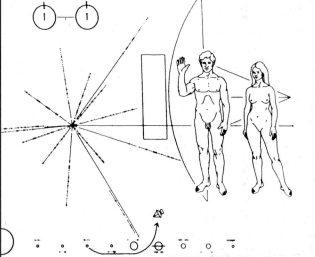

Voyager space probe

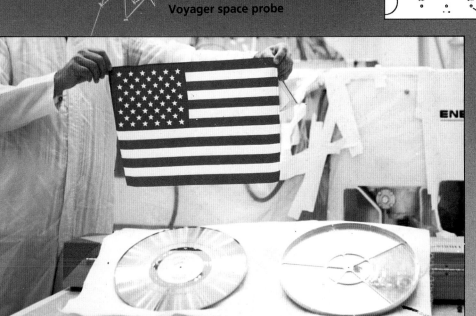

Above: This small plaque is carried aboard both Pioneer space probes. The bottom diagram shows that the craft came from Earth, the third planet from the sun. A man and a woman are shown against an outline of Pioneer to give another intelligent being some idea of how big we are. The man raises his hand in a gesture of peace.

Left: Each Voyager probe carries a gold-plated copper record, complete with stylus in case a passing alien doesn't have a record-player! The disc features music from around the world, along with greetings in 60 languages and the sounds of birds and humpback whales.

Aliens

EACH year people around the world report that they have seen alien spaceships in the sky. In fact, almost all the sightings turn out to be things like meteors, weather balloons, or even the lights of cars on distant hills. But there are always one or two which remain a mystery (these are known as Unidentified Flying Objects or UFOs). Some people claim they have had a closer encounter still, and these reported incidents are put into different groups by UFO researchers. A 'close encounter of the first kind' involves a spaceship landing or deliberately passing close by the person. In a 'close encounter of the second kind' some evidence is left behind, like a scorch mark in the grass from a rocket engine. And if an alien being is actually seen it counts as a 'close encounter of the third kind' (as in the film of the same name).

Above: This photograph was taken by an English schoolboy in Yorkshire in 1966. He claims he actually took a picture of a strange light hovering in the sky . . . and the 'flying saucers' appeared when the film was developed. (Photographs like this one are quite easy to fake and are not proof that UFOs exist.)

Left: Some people see this Italian cave drawing as evidence that aliens visited Earth thousands of years ago. Why else, they ask, would our ancestors have drawn people in 'helmets' with what look like antennae attached?

Above: In recent years, mysterious 'corn circles' like these have appeared each summer in farmers' fields around the world. Although some have been proved to be hoaxes, others remain unexplained – too perfect to be made by trampling down the corn, and without any sign of footsteps leading into the field. Some people suggest they might be caused by a strange, alien force.

Above: Some people who think they have spotted a UFO have in fact witnessed no more than strange-shaped storm clouds. These clouds, looking like 'flying saucers', were photographed in France.

Right: This famous picture of a 'flying saucer' was taken in 1952 by a Californian called George Adamski (above). He claimed the spaceship landed soon after and that he met a Venusian spaceman (who looked quite human but didn't speak English). A few years later, Adamski said he was taken on trips in the spaceship to Venus, Saturn and Jupiter. However, many of the details he gave of the planets have since been proved wrong by the visits of unmanned space probes. As a result most scientists now believe Adamski was a hoaxer and that his photographs were probably faked using models he built himself.

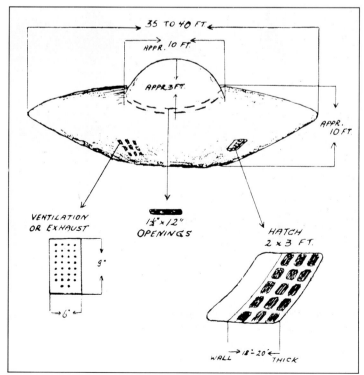

35 TO 40 FT

APPR. 10 FT.

APPR 3 FT.

APPR. 10 FT.

VENTILATION OR EXHAUST

9"

6"

1¾"x12" OPENINGS

HATCH 2 x 3 FT.

WALL 18"-20" THICK

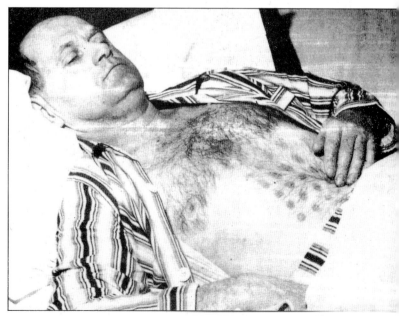

In 1967 a Canadian, Stephen Michalak (above), was admitted to hospital with a strange set of burns on his stomach. He claimed they were caused by getting too close to the exhaust vent of an alien spaceship. His drawing of the UFO is shown left.

Sci-fi: the books

PEOPLE have fantasised about flight and space travel for centuries and their fantasies have produced a rich and colourful literature called 'science fiction' or 'sci-fi'. Its authors and artists are often seen as the creators of impossible dreams, but history has proved that they can provide us with an exciting glimpse of tomorrow's future in space . . . today!

Right: A man flies on an 11-day voyage to the moon with the help of a flock of geese in *The Man on the Moone*, written by the Bishop of Hereford (1638).

Left: Gulliver looks skywards at the flying city of Laputa, powered by a giant magnet, in Jonathan Swift's *Gulliver's Travels* (1726).

Below: A three-man landing on the moon was correctly predicted by Jules Verne, who wrote several science fiction books including *From the Earth to the Moon* (1865) and *Trip Around the Moon* (1870).

Right: Wars between worlds became an increasingly popular theme in sci-fi comics in the 1930s as this front cover of *Startling Stories* (1939) shows.

Above: Two spacemen explore the surface of the moon on this front cover of *Amazing Stories* (1929), one of the most famous sci-fi comics of its time.

Right: The comic-strip character Tintin, created by Hergé in 1929, has introduced space to millions around the world in books like *On a marché sur la Lune* (Explorers on the Moon).

Invaders from Sirius and their daring attempt to steal the Earth is typical of the dramatic stories that featured in *Fantastic Adventures* (1939).

Sci-fi: the movies

SPACE has attracted the attention of Hollywood film-makers and television producers world-wide. In recent years, several space movies including *2001: A Space Odyssey, Star Wars, Alien, Close Encounters of the Third Kind* and, of course, *E.T.* have been 'blockbuster' successes. Television, too, has had its share of success with programmes like *Star Trek*, which led to several feature films, and the BBC's popular *Doctor Who* series.

Above: The crew of a spaceship from Earth on the look-out for danger on a remote planet, in a scene from the movie *Forbidden Planet* which was made in 1956.

Left: Three 'astronauts', interestingly without spacesuits, on the moon in *Frau im Mond* (The Woman in the Moon), directed by Fritz Lang in 1929.

HOWARD KEEL   NICOLE MAUREY
in
THE DAY OF THE TRIFFIDS
Eastman Colour   By Special Arrangement   CinemaScope   Cert. 'X'
JANETTE SCOTT   KIERON MOORE

Paramount Presents
"THE WAR OF THE WORLDS"   Color by TECHNICOLOR   CERT X
Produced by George Pal   Directed by Byron Haskin   Screenplay by Barre Lyndon   Based on the Novel by H. G. Wells

Left: Alien plants from another planet terrorise people on Earth in the film *Day of the Triffids*, directed by Steven Sekely in 1962.

Above: A Martian spaceship leaves a trail of destruction on planet Earth in *War of the Worlds*, written by H. G. Wells in 1898 and turned into a film in 1953.

Left: The starship *Enterprise* is confronted by the evil Klingons' spaceship in a scene from *Star Trek*, the popular television series that developed into several successful Hollywood movies.

Above: A scene from *2001: A Space Odyssey*. The film was directed by Stanley Kubrick and came out in 1968, the year before man finally landed on the moon.

Left: The 'mothership', a huge spaceship city that was home to friendly aliens who visited Planet Earth in Stephen Spielberg's film *Close Encounters of the Third Kind* (1977).

Above: Fearsome storm-troopers prepare to enforce the evil laws of the Emperor of the Galactic Empire in *Star Wars*, directed by George Lucas in 1977.

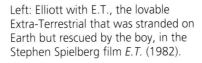

Left: Elliott with E.T., the lovable Extra-Terrestrial that was stranded on Earth but rescued by the boy, in the Stephen Spielberg film *E.T.* (1982).

Space on Earth

THE US Space Camp in Alabama was the first of several space camps that now exist around the world. There are other camps in Florida, Japan and Belgium. The one in Alabama was launched in 1982 and since then more than 100,000 'astronaut trainees', many as young as 10 years old, have earned their 'wings' there. It is based at the Space and Rocket Centre in Huntsville which has the world's biggest collection of rockets on permanent display to the public.

Space camps don't aim to make any money and the space cadets pay only what is needed to cover the costs of their week-long course. Being a cadet at one of these camps is very much a hands-on experience: everyone gets the chance to build and launch a small rocket, try out a wide range of different equipment used to train astronauts and take part in simulated space shuttle missions.

Above: The Space and Rocket Centre in Huntsville, Alabama, has more than 1500 rocket and space exhibits. They include a huge Saturn V rocket, like the one that sent American astronauts to the moon.

Right: Pathfinder, a full-size space shuttle, is one of the main displays in the Shuttle Park at the centre. It is dedicated to the American astronauts who died on the ill-fated Challenger mission in 1986.

Below: The futuristic Space Habitat is home for 444 cadets during their week-long stay at US Space Camp, Alabama. The space-age building is based on designs for America's space station Freedom. Huge metallic tubes run the full length of the Space Habitat, which is longer than a football pitch.

Above: The four floors of the Space Habitat open on to a huge central atrium which is illuminated by skylights in the roof. This main area is used for assemblies and other group activities.

Left: The Space Habitat is divided into six-person 'sleep stations' which contain built-in bunks, exercise equipment, computer work stations and storage compartments.

Above: Stand by for blast-off! Space camps are all about experiencing life as an astronaut. Here, three cadets discover, in a mock-up, what it would have been like in an Apollo capsule – a tight fit!

Space cadets

During their time at a space camp, cadets get the chance to experience a huge variety of space-related activities for themselves – everything from designing a small rocket to building a space station. Some cadets 'fly' the shuttle simulators; some don spacesuits and 'walk in space'; others direct and monitor a flight from Mission Control with the help of computers. They wear copies of astronauts' flight suits, eat space food and also get the chance to try out several pieces of equipment that real astronauts train on.

While one of the main aims of the courses is that the cadets should have fun, there is also an educational side to the space-camp programme. It is hoped that young people will leave the camps with a better understanding of science and space technology, and that some of them might even consider a career in the space industry. Although only very few people are needed to train as astronauts, getting a spacecraft off the ground involves a huge army of engineers, designers and technicians. The chances are that even more of these experts will be needed in the future.

Cadets at the space camps of today might well be working on the space projects of tomorrow – projects like the European manned space flight programme, space station Freedom or the building of permanent bases on the moon, Mars and beyond.

Two space cadets go on a 'space walk' in the shuttle's cargo bay, to repair a damaged communications satellite during a mission simulation. Great efforts are made to ensure that everything is as realistic as possible. Even the spacesuits are based on the real thing.

Trainees get a chance to direct a shuttle flight mission, from take-off through to landing, from a realistically designed Mission Control.

Right: Cadets train in realistic space-shuttle cockpit mock-ups. The commander and pilot use computers to control the spacecraft during simulated space missions, while other trainees carry out experiments.

Above: Two trainees, one of them perched high above the shuttle's payload bay in a manned manoeuvring unit (MMU), start to build a space structure in a simulated exercise.

Above: Another space cadet earns his wings with the hope, maybe, of actually becoming a real shuttle astronaut in a few years time!

Halls of fame

THERE are many museums throughout the world that have departments devoted to space. In addition, there are specially built, permanent exhibitions where visitors can see spacecraft and equipment that has actually travelled to space and back to Planet Earth.

Spaceport USA, Cape Canaveral, Florida, USA

Climb on board Ambassador, a full-size copy of a shuttle at the home of America's space-flight programme: 'The Cape' in Florida. You may even see a real shuttle sitting on the launch pad if you take one of the organised bus tours. And if you're lucky you could watch a launch. Spaceport USA offers a wealth of 'space' experiences indoors and out.

NASA
Visitor Centers

e Small Step

GUIDED TOURS
visit to be more memorable, we suggest
Two different, fascinating tours aboard
onditioned buses featuring taped/live
ra stops are offered at a **nominal fee.**
your tickets at the Ticket
rst arrive. Tours last two
ontinuously
xact routes
e due to
t typically:
'll...
ted launch
where all the
inspect a Saturn V
han a football field
Assembly Building
ldings);
und Crawler
Shuttles to their launch

two pads where ALL
ched and where ALL
ere only by this tour.

Station where the
folds for you;
nauts were
grams;
pads
m-

ce
s one-
issile and
ilia.

A visitors
the crawler
ransporters, an Apollo
lunar module and the Shuttle during launch periods.
▼ IMAX® film presentation

Above: Spaceport USA at Cape Canaveral is one of the major tourist destinations in Florida with displays of spacecraft and equipment.

National Air and Space Museum, Washington DC, USA

There are plenty of space museums in the United States as well as the on-site displays at the main NASA centres in Houston and Cape Canaveral. In this museum you can see the history of space flight on a big scale. Nearly all the craft on display have flown or been on mission stand-by.

Look out for the IMAX cinema where you can see films made by astronauts in space, projected on to a giant screen. *Blue Planet* is about Earth and its delicate environment. *The Dream is Alive* gives you an inside look at the American space-shuttle programme.

Face to face with American astronauts in the museum's Hall of Fame.

to Florida's Final Frontier!

FREE ADMISSION AND PARKING!

KENNEDY SPACE CENTER Spaceport USA
Operated by TW Recreational Services, Inc.

BEST VISITOR VALUE

Where America's Spirit Soars!

Space Expo, Noordwijk, The Netherlands

Have you ever stood underneath a real rocket engine? Ever wanted to look around a space station? The Noordwijk Space Expo invites you to reach out and touch space! It is Europe's first, major, purpose-built space museum. You can be involved in an exciting space quest with the chance of winning an astronaut's diploma. There are models and computer games, and pictures from a weather satellite are transmitted live from space.

The Science Museum, London, United Kingdom

A visit to the Exploration of Space Gallery unlocks many of the secrets of space travel. There are examples of all sorts of spacecraft and gadgetry. In the section on humans in space you can see the spacesuits worn by Apollo astronauts, space food, space underwear – and the Apollo 10 module that flew into space and parachuted back into the sea.

Go for a space walk in Noordwijk, Europe's first museum devoted to the story of space.

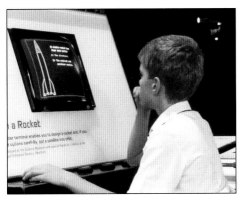

You can design your own rocket, choosing the fuel, payload and weight. Then find out whether it flies!

The Science Museum
(The National Museum of Science and Industry)
Exhibition Road, London SW7 2DD, United Kingdom
Tel: (071) 938 8000

Space Expo
Keplerplaan 3, 2201 AZ Noordwijk, The Netherlands. Tel: (1719) 46 460

National Air and Space Museum (Smithsonian Institution)
6th Street and Independence Avenue, SW Washington DC 20560, USA
Tel: (202) 357 2700

Johnson Space Centre
Nasa Road One, Houston, Texas 77058, USA
Tel: (713) 483 4321

Spaceport USA
Kennedy Space Centre, Florida 32899, USA
Tel: (407) 867 2363

US Space and Rocket Centre
One Tranquility Base, Huntsville, Alabama 35807, USA. Tel: (205) 837 3400. (See p.82.)

Exhibition of Economic Achievements (VDNKh)
Cosmos Pavilion, Prospect Mira, Moscow 129223, Russia. Tel: (095) 943 9801

Question time

What burning question would you ask an American astronaut about travelling to space by shuttle? Here are the answers to some of those things you've always wanted to know . . .

Q What time is it in space?

A Setting your watch in space is a problem. An orbiting craft passes through all of Earth's 24 time-zones every 90 minutes. NASA usually measures time during a shuttle mission by counting from the moment of launch. Everything after that is called 'mission elapsed time' (MET).

Q What is the weather like in space? Is there any wind or movement?

A There is no air in space, so there is no wind, rain or cloud . . . no weather as we know it on Earth. You may have heard of 'the solar wind', but this is the name given to electrical particles that are constantly being thrown out from the sun into space.

Q Are spaceships noisy? Is there any smell?

A When a shuttle blasts off, the main engines and rocket boosters make a terrific noise. After 8½ minutes, once the craft is in orbit and the main engines have been shut off, the only noise comes from the fans that circulate the air.

NASA goes to a lot of trouble to make sure there are no nasty smells in the shuttle. A team of workers carries out 'sniff tests' to make sure nothing that is sent into space smells unpleasant.

Q What does it feel like to blast off? Is it bumpy?

A Astronauts are pushed back into their seats on blast off, just as you are when a car accelerates quickly. But they are on top of a space rocket, so the feeling is much stronger. It is bumpy for the first two minutes after lift-off. Once the rocket boosters have separated from the craft the ride gets much smoother. In orbit, when the main engines are shut off, there is absolutely no feeling of movement.

Q Can astronauts eat and drink when they like? Is it difficult?

A NASA's space-meal chefs come up with a menu of about 70 different foods and 20 different drinks for astronauts to choose from before they leave. They can eat snacks and drink whenever they like, but each crew member is set three specific times for breakfast, lunch and dinner.

The chefs make sure there are no loose pieces of food that might escape in the weightless conditions of space. It could be dangerous if an astronaut accidentally inhaled a bit of floating bread or biscuit!

Q Does the world look polluted from space?

A Yes. Astronauts can see air pollution and oil spills and the atmosphere sometimes looks 'dirty', usually when there has been an event like a volcanic eruption. They can also see smoke plumes from fires in the rainforests of South America. At other times, the atmosphere looks clear.

Q What man-made objects on Earth can be seen from space? Is it true that astronauts can see the Great Wall of China?

A When astronauts are in orbit they can see things like airports and cities. Using an ordinary pair of binoculars they can pick out roads and parks. No one has ever reported seeing the Great Wall of China from space – it's a myth!

Q What is the most unusual thing about being in space?

A The weirdest aspect of space travel is the feeling of weightlessness. What astronauts most enjoy is the amazing view of Planet Earth.

SPACE LOG

4 October 1957

USSR launched the world's first satellite: Sputnik 1. (*Sputnik* means 'travelling companion'.) A radio transmitter inside the aluminium ball sent a 'bleep bleep' signal which was picked up on Earth. All around the world people looked out for the little satellite as it passed over them in the night sky.

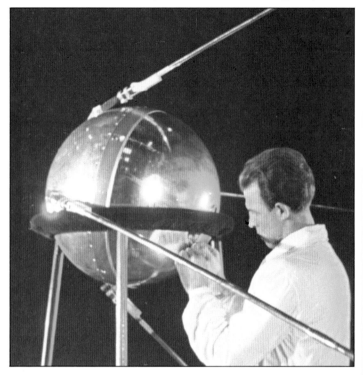

3 November 1957

USSR launched Sputnik 2. It carried the first live passenger into space – a mongrel dog called Laika. This time the space capsule was shaped like a cone, with a pressurised cabin for Laika. Sadly, she died during the flight.

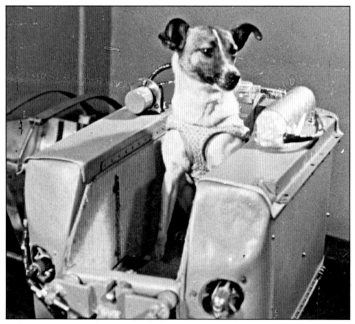

18 May 1959

Miss Baker and fellow 'monkeynaut' Able became the first primates launched into space by the United States and recovered alive.

4 October 1959

USSR launched Luna 3. It went into orbit around the moon and sent back the first-ever photographs of the far side, or dark side, of the moon – the part you can't see from Earth.

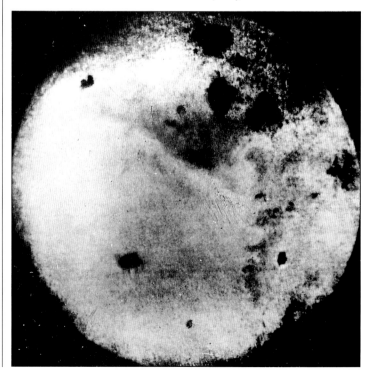

12 April 1961

USSR launched the first person into space: Yuri Gagarin aboard Vostok 1. He orbited the Earth once – it took 1 hour 48 minutes – before returning safely to a hero's welcome. He never went into space again.

5 May 1961

USA launched the first American into space: Alan B. Shepherd. He did not actually orbit the Earth, but returned after 15 minutes. The mission was broadcast live on television.

20 February 1962

USA launched the first American into orbit: John Glenn, in his capsule Friendship 7. He made three Earth orbits in a space flight lasting nearly five hours. Once again, the whole mission was seen live on television.

10 July 1962

USA launched the first in a series of communications satellites: Telstar 1. It made history by transmitting the first live television pictures from North America across the Atlantic Ocean to Europe.

27 August 1962

USA launched Mariner 2 on the first mission to explore another planet in our solar system. On 14 December 1962, 109 days later, the craft flew past Venus, sending back information about the planet's surface temperature. Three weeks later all Earth contact with Mariner 2 was lost.

16 June 1963

USSR launched the first woman in space: Valentina Tereshkova. She orbited the Earth 48 times over three days, aboard Vostok 6.

18 March 1965

Soviet cosmonaut Alexei Leonov went for the first-ever walk in space, attached by an air tube to his spacecraft Voskhod 2. It lasted 12 minutes. Leonov had trouble getting back into the airlock of his spacecraft, because his spacesuit had expanded during the walk.

3 June 1965

USA astronaut Ed White made the first space walk by an American. He spent more than 20 minutes outside his spacecraft Gemini 4. The 'umbilical cord' connecting him to the capsule supplied him with oxygen, and he held a rocket gun which he fired to help him move around in the vacuum of space.

21 December 1968

USA launched the first people to orbit the moon in Apollo 8. They sent back the first live television pictures of the lunar surface, thrilling an audience of millions around the world at Christmas.

16 July 1969

USA launched Apollo 11 on the world's first mission to land people on the moon. Astronauts Neil Armstrong and Buzz (Edwin) Aldrin made the first human footprints on the lunar surface on 20 July (see p. 14). Again, millions of people were glued to their television screens, no matter what time of the night or day it was in their part of the world, to watch those pictures 'live from the moon'.

2 March 1972

USA launched Pioneer 10, a space probe with the mission of flying past Jupiter and photographing the planet. Pioneer 10 also became the first object sent from Earth to leave our solar system – a 10-year flight. It is still hurtling through space to this day!

7 December 1972

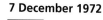

USA launched Apollo 17, the last spacecraft to land people on the moon. The mission broke many records: at 12 days, it was the longest Apollo mission; it stayed the longest time on the moon – 75 hours; the moon buggy was used to travel further than before, and a record number of moon samples were brought back to Earth.

14 May 1973

USA launched Skylab 1, America's first manned, orbiting space station (see p. 36). It was equipped with scientific instruments to carry out tests automatically. Visiting crews, each consisting of three astronauts, could perform dozens of experiments, particularly on each other to find out how well the human body copes with space travel.

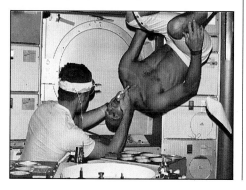

17 July 1975

Space travellers from America and the Soviet Union docked their spacecraft together in a gesture of friendship – the two countries had previously been rivals in the space race. The Apollo-Soyuz Test Project was a one-off combined mission. US astronauts 'Deke' Slayton (left) and Tom Stafford (right) and Soviet cosmonaut Alexei Leonov, shook hands, spoke each other's languages and performed experiments together.

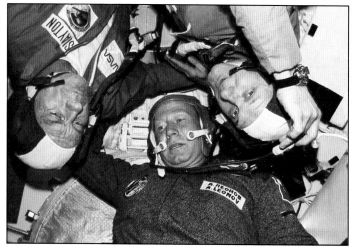

24 December 1979

Europe launched the first Ariane rocket from its space port in French Guiana, South America. The Christmas Eve unmanned mission was a complete success.

12 April 1981

USA launched the first space shuttle, Columbia, 20 years to the day after Yuri Gagarin went into space. The world's first re-usable spacecraft, crewed by John Young and Robert Crippen, orbited 36 times before landing safely back on Earth. (See also p. 20.)

24 June 1982

The French *spationaut* Jean-Loup Chrétien became the first European in space. He travelled aboard the USSR's Soyuz T-6 to visit the space station Salyut 7.

18 June 1983

USA launched the first American woman in space. Dr Sally Ride flew on board Challenger on the seventh shuttle flight.

7 February 1984

American astronaut Bruce McCandless became the first person to space-walk without an 'umbilical cord' attaching him to his spacecraft. He was the first to use the manned manoeuvring unit (MMU), which also made him the first human satellite, orbiting Earth for more than an hour.

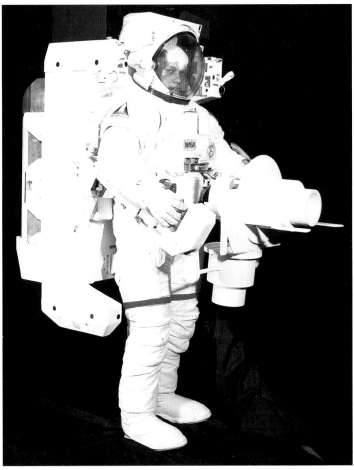

9 April 1984

Astronauts from space shuttle Challenger performed a tricky operation to 'catch' a faulty satellite known as Solar Max. They repaired it in Challenger's cargo bay, then released it back into orbit to continue its study of solar flares. (See p. 58.)

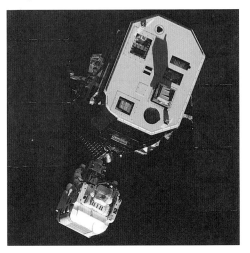

17 July 1984

Cosmonaut Svetlana Savitskaya became the first female space-walker. It was her second time in space and she travelled on Soyuz T-12.

28 January 1986

USA's shuttle Challenger blew up 73 seconds after launch. All seven crew were killed, including the schoolteacher Christa McAuliffe who was to have taught American school-children direct from space. (See also p. 54.)

19 February 1986

USSR launched the main part of a permanent space station called Mir. (*Mir* means 'peace'.) It can be visited by several spacecraft at the same time, and new modules can be added to make it bigger and better equipped. (See also p. 38.)

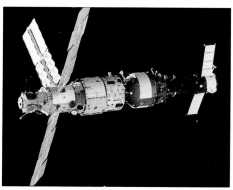

15 November 1988

USSR launched its space shuttle Buran. (*Buran* means 'snowstorm'.) Its maiden launch was unmanned, and after orbiting Earth twice it returned safely back home. Manned launches are planned for 1994–95. Another photograph of Buran is on p. 23.

21 December 1988

Soviet cosmonauts Vladimir Titov and Musa Manarov completed a record-breaking whole year in space, living on board space station Mir. They were not always on their own – other crews sometimes came to stay.

18 May 1991

Britain's first cosmonaut, Helen Sharman, blasted off in the Soviet Union's Soyuz T-12. She carried out experiments on board space station Mir.

Index

Picture credits
Key: l – left, r – right, t – top, c – centre, b – bottom, tl – top left, tc – top centre, tr – top right, bc – bottom centre, bl – bottom left, br – bottom right, cl – centre left, cr – centre right)
We would like to thank Mike Gentry of NASA Lyndon B. Johnson Space Center, Houston for all his help. In addition BBC Books would like to thank the following for providing photographs, and for permission to reproduce copyright material. While every effort has been made to trace and acknowledge all copyright holders, we would like to apologise should there have been any errors or omissions.
Arianespace/ESA 62 (l); **BAE/ESA** 62 (tr); **Bibliothèque de l'Institut des Hautes Etudes Chinoises**, College de France, Paris 8 (bl); **British Library** 78 (tr); **CNES/SPOT IMAGE/EXPLORER** 46 (bl); **ESA** 42 (br), 49 (br), 62/63, 63 (r), 93 (br); **ESA/ERS-1** 45 (br); **Hergé/Casterman** 79 (br); **Hulton Deutsch Collection** 90 (br); **ISAS** 64 (t); **ISRO** 65 (t); **Kennedy Space Center**, Spaceport USA 86/87 (t); **KOBAL/© Paramount** 81 (tl); **Mary Evans Picture Library** 76 (tr), 76 (bl), 76 (br), 77 (br), 78 (tl), 78 (bl), 78 (bc), 78 (br), 79 (tl, tr, bl); by courtesy of the **National Portrait Gallery**, London 9 (bl); **NASA for ESA** 1, 40 (t); **National Air and Space Museum**, Smithsonian Institution, Washington 9 (tl), 9 (r), 86 (b); **Noordwijk Space Expo** 87 (c); **Novosti** 14 (tr), 23 (br), 55 (cr), 55 (br), 90 (bl), 91 (tl), 91 (tc), 91 (cl), 92 (tl), 92 (cl), 94 (cl), 95 (bl); **OPEL** 8 (t); **Pictorial Press/© 20th Century Fox** 81 (br); **Rutherford Appleton Laboratory** 43 (t); **Science Museum**, London 8 (bc), 87 (bl); **Science Photo Library** 6 (t), 11 (l), 38 (b), 49 (br), 95 (tr); **Sygma** 39 (tr); **Tass** 35 (b), 38/39, 38 (t), 39 (bl), 39 (tr), 57 (br), 90 (tl), 95 (tl), 95 (cr), 95 (c), 95 (br); **The Ronald Grant Archive/© MGM** 80 (t), 81 (tr); **The Ronald Grant Archive/© Paramount** 80 (br); **The Ronald Grant Archive/© Columbia Pictures** 81 (c); **The Ronald Grant Archive** 80 (c), 80 (bl); **© 1982 Universal City Studios/Stephen Spielberg** 5 (bl), 81 (bl); **US Department of Defence** 47 (tl), 47 (tc), 47 (tr); **U.S. Space Camp®** 5 (bc), 82/83, 84/85, 90 (tr); by courtesy of the Board of Trustees of the **Victoria and Albert Museum**, London 8 (br). All remaining pictures © NASA.
Illustrators: David A. Hardy; Mike Roffe; Philip Roberts; Peter Utton; Graham White.